Designing and Building
Enterprise Knowledge Graphs

Synthesis Lectures on Data, Semantics, and Knowledge

Editor
Ying Ding, *University of Texas at Austin*
Paul Groth, *University of Amsterdam*

Founding Editor Emeritus
James Hendler, *Rensselaer Polytechnic Institute*

Synthesis Lectures on Data, Semantics, and Knowledge is edited by Ying Ding of the University of Texas at Austin and Paul Groth of the University of Amsterdam. The series focuses on the pivotal role that data on the web and the emergent technologies that surround it play both in the evolution of the World Wide Web as well as applications in domains requiring data integration and semantic analysis. The large-scale availability of both structured and unstructured data on the Web has enabled radically new technologies to develop. It has impacted developments in a variety of areas including machine learning, deep learning, semantic search, and natural language processing. Knowledge and semantics are a critical foundation for the sharing, utilization, and organization of this data. The series aims both to provide pathways into the field of research and an understanding of the principles underlying these technologies for an audience of scientists, engineers, and practitioners.

Topics to be included:

- Knowledge graphs, both public and private

- Linked Data

- Knowledge graph and automated knowledge base construction

- Knowledge engineering for large-scale data

- Machine reading

- Uses of Semantic Web technologies

- Information and knowledge integration, data fusion

- Various forms of semantics on the web (e.g., ontologies, language models, and distributional semantics)

- Terminology, Thesaurus, & Ontology Management

- Query languages

Designing and Building Enterprise Knowledge Graphs

Juan Sequeda and Ora Lassila

ISBN: 978-3-031-00788-0   paperback
ISBN: 978-3-031-01916-6   ebook
ISBN: 978-3-031-00111-6   hardcover

DOI 10.1007/978-3-031-01916-6

A Publication in the Springer series
SYNTHESIS LECTURES ON DATA, SEMANTICS, AND KNOWLEDGE

Lecture #20
Series Editors: Ying Ding, *University of Texas at Austin*
                        Paul Groth, *University of Amsterdam*
Founding Editor Emeritus: James Hendler, *Rensselaer Polytechnic Institute*
Series ISSN
Print 2691-2023   Electronic 2691-2031

Designing and Building Enterprise Knowledge Graphs

Juan Sequeda
data.world

Ora Lassila
Amazon

SYNTHESIS LECTURES ON DATA, SEMANTICS, AND KNOWLEDGE #20

ABSTRACT

This book is a guide to designing and building knowledge graphs from enterprise relational databases in practice. It presents a principled framework centered on mapping patterns to connect relational databases with knowledge graphs, the roles within an organization responsible for the knowledge graph, and the process that combines data and people. The content of this book is applicable to knowledge graphs being built either with property graph or RDF graph technologies.

Knowledge graphs are fulfilling the vision of creating intelligent systems that integrate knowledge and data at large scale. Tech giants have adopted knowledge graphs for the foundation of next-generation enterprise data and metadata management, search, recommendation, analytics, intelligent agents, and more. We are now observing an increasing number of enterprises that seek to adopt knowledge graphs to develop a competitive edge.

In order for enterprises to design and build knowledge graphs, they need to understand the critical data stored in relational databases. How can enterprises successfully adopt knowledge graphs to integrate data and knowledge, without boiling the ocean? This book provides the answers.

KEYWORDS

knowledge graphs, data integration, enterprise data management, ontologies, semantic web, graph databases, relational databases, semantic technologies, property graph, RDF graph

This book is dedicated to the early adopters who believed in the idea of knowledge graphs from the beginning, have been trying to deploy knowledge graphs in practice (successfully and sometimes not), and have to grapple with folks with different and divergent thoughts about knowledge graphs. You fought the uphill battle against people resistant to change, and you continue to persevere. Thank you! You know who you are!

Contents

Preface

Here, we try to answer the simple question: Why did we write this book?

Every organization has problems with data. If you say your organization does not, you are either fooling yourself or you are not paying attention. While there are many problems with "modern" data practice, in this book we will focus on the fact that *data* and *knowledge* are by and large disconnected, and we want to report on our long quest to connect the two (spoiler: knowledge graphs will bring relief to this).

Please understand that this is an *opinionated* book, based on our own experience in designing and building knowledge graph systems and helping others do the same. Ora was a co-author of the original W3C RDF specification from 1997, and co-authored the seminal *Scientific American* article on the Semantic Web in 2001. Juan has transfered technology (from a university research project to production in various enterprises) that integrates relational databases with Semantic Web technologies. We have particpated in numerous projects (successful and sometimes not so successful) in domains such as e-commerce, finance, energy, and pharmaceutical. We truly believe that knowledge graphs are the ideal way of managing enterprise data because of the capabilities of connecting knowledge and data at scale.

Knowledge graphs are "hot" right now, and thus we see a lot of people jumping on the knowledge graph bandwagon without necessarily understanding how to leverage these new technologies. And funny enough, everyone is talking about "semantics" without understanding what that term really *means*. Time and again, we see companies get excited about knowledge graphs, jump to the conclusion that it is simply the same thing as a graph database, and roll up their sleeves without applying a principled framework of how to design and build a knowledge graph. We have seen people use graph databases without considering modeling questions. We have seen people believe that AI can automate everything. Without a principled, well thought-out approach, many organizations go about their knowledge graph projects in haphazard, ad hoc manner. We want to avoid early adopters getting *too excited*, jumping into the deep end, and possibly drowning due to the lack of a principled framework and guidelines. What we would like to avoid is some kind of "knowledge graph winter" (cf. AI winter), a backlash against these promising technologies that could happen if enough people attempt adoption without a clear, principled approach. This book is the result of our lessons learned, and provides a framework that works in practice within the enterprise.

The focus of this book is on relational databases as a source of the knowledge graph. A vast amount of knowledge graph literature is based on the assumption of automating the creation of a knowledge graph from unstructured data (text) and semi-structured data (web pages, web tables, open data, logs, etc). These are very challenging problems that Tech Giants and the FAANG companies (Facebook, Amazon, Apple, Netflix, Google) encounter. Various comprehensive surveys and books have been published on this topic. However, not all organizations have the same challenges as the tech giants. The majority of critical data resides in relational databases that power applications such as Customer Relationship Management (CRM), Enterprise Resource Planning (ERP), and Order Management Systems (OMS). Furthermore, data warehouses are specialized relational databases. While data lakes enable storage of semi-structured data, the main ways of access are through SQL interfaces. There is a lack of literature that focuses on the day-to-day problems that organizations face when building knowledge graphs from their main type of source: relational databases. This book aims to fill that gap.

We think that if you are reading this book, you already want to leverage graph technologies. If in your mind the question of "relational vs. graph" is still at the forefront, you may not be ready for this book. Don't be one of those people!

The goal of our book is to offer a principled framework as well as guidance that combines people, processes, and technology to build and design enterprise knowledge graphs from relational databases. The book is structured in the following manner.

1. We introduce graphs, giving you some background as well as motivating examples why the "old ways" may not work so well. The last skeptics will now become believers.

2. We discuss design of knowledge graphs.

3. We give you a set of *mapping patterns* that let you move from relational to graphs. You need this library.

4. Not everything can be automated, so we help you build your knowledge graphs by explaining that to do this, you need *people*, a *process*, and *tools*. The people part is important here, as you must understand what roles are needed in a modern knowledge graph practice.

5. At the end, a brief look into the future and some final words of wisdom.

   Welcome and good luck! We are glad you are here.

Juan Sequeda and Ora Lassila
July 2021

Foreword by an Anonymous CDO

Much has been written about the growth of data. You may be familiar with the hockey stick charts or statements that the vast majority of data was created in the last few years. This has driven one of the single largest gold rushes we've seen. The market cap of data- and AI-related companies now measure in the trillions of dollars.

As we all know, this data often remains untouched or underutilized. The greatest challenge with using this data stems from processing large swathes of unstructured data and then connecting both structured and unstructured data together for use.

Knowledge graphs, along with supplemental technologies such as natural language processing and entity resolution, are at the heart of managing and making use of this new data. Leading AI companies such as Google, Microsoft, and Amazon use these approaches to help process billions of websites and to produce the greatest e-commerce catalog ever known. While most enterprises do not process anywhere near the volume of data as these tech companies, they can learn from these Data and AI leaders on better utilizing and managing their data.

Knowledge graphs represent a significant shift for the enterprise—connecting data together, in a common and understandable way, to scale the adoption and use of data. It holds the promise of breaking silos, democratizing use of data, harvesting insights from all types of data (both structured and unstructured), and accelerating data agility (the speed by which you can utilize and act on your data). Moreover, knowledge graphs can usher in the development of a data product eco-system within an organization, modeling and connecting data to represent how your business operates. For example, knowledge graphs can power the development of data products such as Customer or Employee 360s, building data products that stitch together dozens to hundreds of sources and create a common approach to expose it for use. No longer do data consumers need to find raw sources and re-integrate them together; they access their data via these well versioned and managed products. Better yet, this technology builds upon the existing investments on data storage and management capabilities already in place—including data lakes and cloud data warehouse efforts. Those who get it right, will have a significant edge over others on application of their data.

Both Juan and Ora have been pioneers in the knowledge graph space. Between them, they have spent well over four decades shaping this space, publishing research on its use, building community of practitioners, understanding organizational implications, and also applying it in real life situations. Ora is leading efforts now at Amazon to bring knowledge graphs to the masses via their Neptune offering and Juan is leading knowledge graph efforts at data.world, which is acting as a data catalog that enables organizations to build knowledge graphs on top of their data. I am always excited to speak with both of them, and learn about where the technologies have been deployed and how to get it right.

If data is like electricity, then the knowledge graph is the grid of the future, and Ora and Juan are building the blueprints.

Anonymous CDO
July 2021

Foreword by Tom Plasterer

At the start of the 2019 inaugural Knowledge Graph Conference (KGC) at Columbia University, I had one question: "What is a knowledge graph?" Not that I didn't have some understanding of the term *knowledge graph* as I've been a champion in the life sciences, but I was really interested to see how we as a broad, cross-domain community think about knowledge graphs and their utility.

By way of training, I'm a bioinformatician and systems biologist. As such, one of the main challenges we have is how understand big, heterogeneous, fast, and messy datasets assembled to better understand key biological questions from basic research to public health.

Life science organizations were among the first adopters of graph approaches as a way of harmonizing our datasets. For biologists, a graph is both a natural way to think about your data with all of its varying data types, relationships, and levels of hierarchy as well as a useful way to organize and structure it. Consider that you can model as a graph a biochemical reaction, a biological pathway, pharmacodynamics, and much more.

We first adopted the term *semantic web*, based on the Resource Description Framework (RDF), then *linked data* and now *FAIR (Findable, Accessible, Interoperable, Reusable) data*—although FAIR data doesn't necessarily presume an RDF foundation. From a life science perspective, a knowledge graph is really the ultimate use for FAIR data. You have an expressive, self-describing data model accompanied with instance data that can then be used to solve real problems, with provenance.

Back to the 2019 KGC and my opening question: this was, to the best of my knowledge, the first-time knowledge graph experts from across life sciences, technology, commerce, transportation, hospitality, energy, entertainment, and government came together to describe their approaches. Many groups used RDF-based graphs and just as many others used property graphs. Over the course of the next two Knowledge Graph Conferences, we came to see interoperability between both approaches starting to prevail. For some, use cases and an RDF-based approach clearly made sense, while others benefited from property graphs. Both fit under the broad umbrella of knowledge graphs, but how you intend to consume the graph will determine what implementation makes sense for your use case. You can have property graph principles in an RDF graph and RDF graph principles in a property graph. So, if the challenge isn't whether you can annotate an edge or whether you can wrap sets of edges into a subgraph, what is it?

I'd say it is that the vast majority of the world's data is stored in text, tables, spreadsheets, relational databases, and other forms that tend to be closed containers. So how do we unlock them and make them behave as if they're part of a harmonized knowledge graph? This is where the use of common vocabularies, common identifiers, and the semantic mapping approaches can help.

Our esteemed guides Ora Lassila and Juan Sequeda have spent their careers working on these challenges. Ora is one of the co-founders of this semantic web while Juan determined how to make relational databases behave as knowledge graphs. Both have played key roles in maturing the underlying knowledge graph technology stack as well as nurturing the broader knowledge graph community. Here, they present a practical guide to unite people, business process, and tools using knowledge graphs to solve real problems out of data you already have at hand. I'll also leave it to Juan and Ora to define a knowledge graph more clearly than I can.

Tom Plasterer, Ph.D.
Data Strategy Lead
Oncology Translational Medicine
AstraZeneca
July 2021

Acknowledgments

Juan says: My knowledge graph journey has been possible thanks to many people. I am lucky to have been exposed to the semantic web early on by Oscar Corcho at a seminar he gave at the Universidad del Valle in Cali, Colombia. I then met Prof. Dan Miranker as an undergrad at UT Austin who asked me a basic question: what's the relationship between relational databases and semantic web? That question changed my life and became the focus of my undergraduate and doctoral research. Dan always pushed me to strive for excellence. The answer we found to that question became the basis of the startup we both founded: Capsenta. Thanks to all of our customers that led to the learnings presented in this book. I'm thankful for everyone at Capsenta and Wayne Heideman's mentorship to learn how to take research and apply it to the real world which led to the acquisition of Capsenta by data.world. I'm fortunate to be supported by data.world and Bryon Jacob where we share a mission and vision on knowledge graphs. Finally, thanks to my family for always being there for me and especially my wife for being my writing partner.

Ora says: I am indebted to all the people who have influenced my thinking and helped me during my long knowledge graph "journey:" my late thesis advisor, Professor Markku Syrjänen (who always used to say "an expert is a person who does not have to think, because he knows"), my former colleagues at Nokia, W3C, and State Street; and especially my current Neptune graph database colleagues and customers. Finally, I'd like to thank my daughter Lauren Lassila, who many years ago, at age 7, insisted that I explain to her what my doctoral thesis was about. Knowledge graphs and semantic modeling can be understood by 7-year-olds!

We would also like to thank those people who read our early manuscript and offered helpful advice and corrections: Charles Ivie (AWS), Tim Gasper (data.world), and the editors Ying Ding and Paul Groth.

Finally, we wouldn't be here if it weren't for the entire Semantic Web community: the various W3C Working Groups, numerous academic research groups, open-source software developers, and commercial product vendors who all have embraced this technology.

Juan Sequeda and Ora Lassila
July 2021

Disclaimer

This is an opinionated book based on our experiences of designing and building enterprise knowledge graphs in practice. Additionally, the focus of this book is on relational databases as a source of the knowledge graph.

CHAPTER 1

Introduction

Enterprise data management needs to evolve. Consider the following example:

"The Van Buren Bank has felt the effects of deregulation which made the once stable banking industry highly competitive. With the decreased spread between borrowing and lending rates, profits on loans have dwindled, making profit on services to customers critical. In the corporate banking group, account managers who in the past could concentrate only on loan volumes must now focus on customer and product profitability. This means they must make decisions differently and need different kinds of information. For example, if a long-time customer threatens to take his or her business elsewhere unless he or she is given an unusually low interest loan, the account manager must decide whether this is an otherwise profitable customer in terms of his or her total business with the bank.

In order to determine how profitable a customer is, the account manager must gather information about the various products and services the customer buys and the profitability of each. Conceptually this could be done by communicating with other account managers around the world who also do business with this customer (or communicating with their electronically readable records) and consolidating the information.

However, it may or may not be true that the customer is identified in the same way in each account manager's records; or that the various products and services the bank sells are identified the same way or grouped into the same categories; or that the size of each account is recorded in the same currency; or that discounts, refunds, and so forth are handled in the same way. The account manager must translate all this information from many sources into a common form and determine how profitable this customer is.

Unfortunately, at the Van Buren Bank, all customer identifiers were typically assigned by the branches and were not standard across the bank. Therefore, there was no way to identify all the business of a given customer short of phoning up every branch and asking. It was clear that the Van Buren Bank required much more data integration than was currently built into its information systems."

This example is an excerpt from a 1992 paper [Goodhue et al., 1992]![1] The example hits the nail on the head on the struggles that enterprises still go through today, 30 years later.

---

[1] The mention of deregulation should have been a hint that this was not a modern example.

It is clear that enteprise data management needs to evolve in a way that data and knowledge are connected, where real-world concepts and relationshps are at the forefront instead of the complex and inscrutable application database schemas. This can now be accomplished with a technology called *knowledge graphs*: integrating knowledge and data at scale where the real world concepts and relationships are first class citizens. The data happens to be represented in a graph. Why? Read on...

Graphs are a new way to look at data. Not truly "new," because these technologies have been around for several decades, or centuries even if you think of mathematics and graph theory. They are new, however, in the sense that graph technologies are only now moving into the mainstream information systems practice, and thus many people are newly exposed to them. While graphs, in the abstract, are a very intuitive and natural way to represent information and to model the world, graph databases per se are different from traditional ways in which we model and manage data. The industry has almost half a century of experience with relational databases and the relational model, and thus the tooling, methods, educational curricula, etc., are all geared toward this. *"The limits of my language mean the limits of my world"*[2] very much applies here: SQL is the language, and thus understanding that there are other ways to do things, ways not even possible with SQL, makes it hard for many people to get started with graphs or to understand how they could use graphs to their benefit and advantage. This can make it hard to adopt graphs.

We will revisit the question of "why are things hard?" in more detail later in the book, but before we start building actual knowledge graphs, we will introduce some background. While the term "knowledge graph" was really introduced into the mainstream vocabulary less than a decade ago (by Google[3]), the idea is much older, and there is easily over half a century of research and software work that preceded what now seems to be a "hot" new concept in the world of enterprise information systems [Gutierrez and Sequeda, 2021].

We can look at knowledge graphs from two, somewhat related, angles: First, there is the practical question of *how to manage and exploit all the information modern enterprises collect and store*. Second, there is the more theoretical question of *how to represent and structure information about the real world*. While the first question is something all CIOs today are pondering, and the second question is something that indeed predates computers altogether, the two are inextricably linked, and we will discuss how knowledge graphs are the embodiment of solutions and answers to both questions.

1.1   WHAT IS THE PROBLEM?

In a modern enterprise, the critical data is stored in a relational database.[4] There are several roles that could collectively be described as *data consumers*. These include data analysts, data scientists, as well as others who must find answers to critical business questions (say, to optimize

---

[2] *"Die Grenzen meiner Sprache bedeuten die Grenzen meiner Welt"*—Ludwig Wittgenstein, 1922.
[3] https://blog.google/products/search/introducing-knowledge-graph-things-not/
[4] Even though modern data lakes are not implemented using relational databases, they provide a SQL interface for access.

business decisions) and deliver these answers as accurately and as quickly as possible. To be able to deliver, the data consumers need access to data stored in relational databases. What we hope to demonstrate in this book is that "*accessible data*" does not only consist of the physical bits stored in an enterprise information system (and the associated credentials for one to get their hands on said bits). In order to truly access data, one also needs to understand how the data is logically structured and, most importantly, **what it means**. The main obstacle to delivering the business answers is specifically the lack of understanding of the meaning of the data. Throughout this book, we will thus employ the idea that

accessible data = physical bits + semantics

And by "semantics" we refer to the *meaning* of the physical bits—this will be discussed in a later section.

In an organization, the roles such as data engineers, data architects, and data stewards can be categorized as *data producers*. They typically are the "high clergy" entrusted with defining, structuring, and managing data. They are the ones who understand the complex database schemas that are the prerequisite for data access. Problems arise because of the communication difficulties between the data consumers and the data producers; this may be due to lack of agreed terminology or indeed simply because of the limits of human communication. Data consumers must communicate to the data producers what it is that they want; instead, our ultimate goal should be to encourage and empower the consumers to access data, perform queries, and generate reports on their own, with nominal support of data producers, thus reducing effort and time, and minimizing the chance for errors. We think of this as "democratizing" enterprise data.

Unfortunately, the current ways of solving this general problem are painstaking and complex in their own right. Below, we will discuss these.

1.1.1 SPREADSHEET APPROACH

A data analyst needs to answer a business question and asks a data engineer for some data. Once the data engineer starts to gather the data they realize that it's a bit more complex and that they need to talk to the data architect who is the expert in the system (Figure 1.1). However, the data architect is very busy and may take days to answer. Finally, the data engineer gets the needed clarifications, comes up with the SQL query that returns the data which is then sent as a CSV or Excel file to the data analyst by email.

The data analyst takes the data and does some additional calculations in Excel and generates a report. This entire process can take days or even weeks.

The situation continues: the data analyst just got the data as a particular snapshot in time and needs to get an updated version of the data every week or every day. Additionally, the data analyst goes through this cycle with different data engineers, generating several spreadsheets of data. Technically savvy data analysts may have a (unofficial) database on their computer from

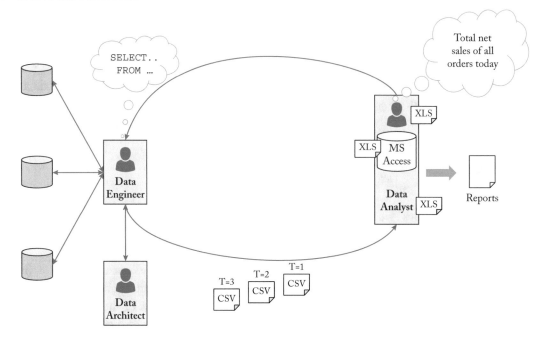

Figure 1.1: Spreadsheet approach.

which they can export a spreadsheet (MS Access is common) and this makes it much easier to "munge" the data together.

Finally, where is the data being integrated? On the data analyst's laptop!

This leaves us with some open questions.

- Did the data analyst communicate the correct request to the data engineer?

- Did the data engineer correctly understand what the data analyst required?

- Did the data engineer deliver the correct and precise results?

- They may have understood correctly, but the SQL query could have been incorrect.

1.1.2   QUERY APPROACH

In this scenario, the data engineer is tired of running a query and simply sending the results to the data analyst. Therefore, the data engineer provides the data analyst with read-only access to the database and gives them the SQL query to execute. Given the complexity of the database, these are often complicated queries that the data analyst does not understand and thus are treated as "black boxes" (Figure 1.2).

Similar to the Spreadsheet approach, the data analyst may receive a variety of SQL queries from different data engineers. A technically savvy data analyst is able to combine the different SQL queries into a one large query by joining each query as a subquery, assuming the queries are all to the same database:

```
SELECT *
FROM (sql query 1) A
JOIN (sql query 2) B ON A.ID = B.ID
JOIN (sql query 2) C ON B.ID = C.ID
...
```

Often, the data analyst will extract the calculations from the spreadsheet and push them into the SQL query. These calculations can contain important business definitions and are pushed into the black box. This entire process is complicated, can easily get out of hand, and that is why you can see queries that are pages long and intelligible only to a few experts in an organization.

Again, we have some open questions.

- Who actually understands what these SQL queries are doing?

- Were the joins performed on the correct keys?

- Can we trust the results of these queries?

1.1.3 DATA WAREHOUSE APPROACH

Enterprise Data Warehouses (EDWs) are a general solution used to integrate data from various disparate sources, for the purposes of data analysis and business decision-making [Inmon, 2005] (Figure 1.3). Based on our experience and anecdotal evidence, projects to build an EDW are often quoted to take "6 months and $1 million USD" but can take 2–3 times longer, and even then they may not be successful.[5] A team (sometimes an IT consultancy company) will gather requirements from all the business stakeholders to design an enterprise data model that covers all the requirements, and to understand what data is needed. A team of data engineers will write ETL code to extract the data from the sources, translate it into the enterprise data model, and then load it into the data warehouse. This follows a "boil the ocean" approach. Once the data is centralized in the warehouse, data analysts can access a single source instead of having to go through the previous spreadsheet and query approaches.

A common follow-up scenario is that either a requirement was misunderstood—hence the data is wrong—or a requirement was missing—and hence data is missing. This means that the

---

[5]This is based on anecdotes but is commonly agreed upon by industry professionals. We encourage the reader to ask around.

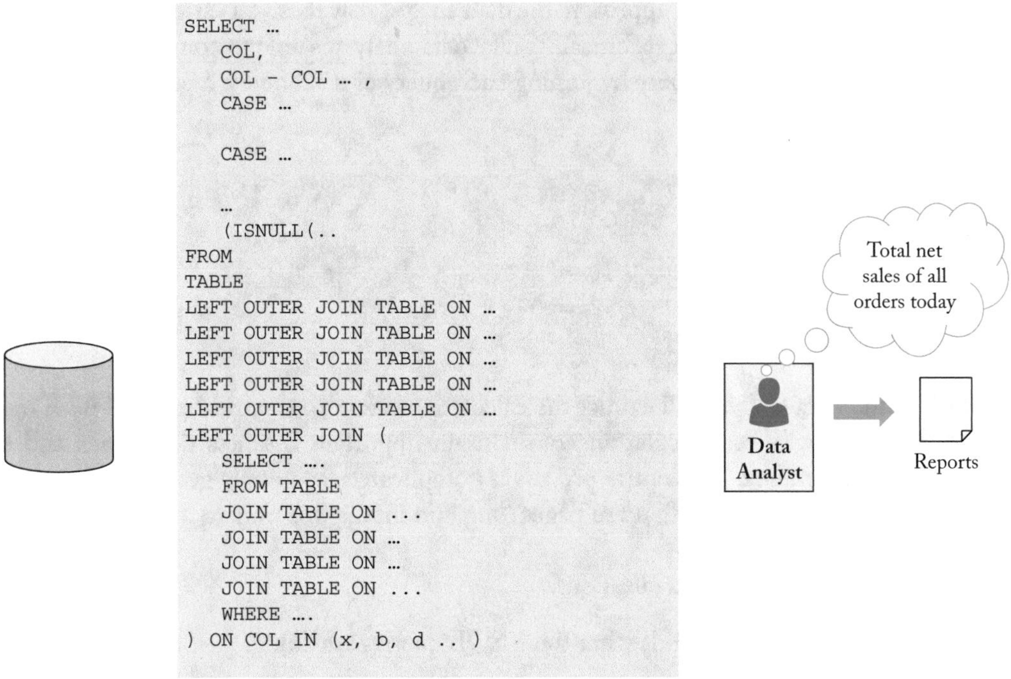

```
SELECT ...
    COL,
    COL - COL ... ,
    CASE ...

    CASE ...


    ...
    (ISNULL(..
FROM
TABLE
LEFT OUTER JOIN TABLE ON ...
LEFT OUTER JOIN TABLE ON ...
LEFT OUTER JOIN TABLE ON ...
LEFT OUTER JOIN TABLE ON ...
LEFT OUTER JOIN TABLE ON ...
LEFT OUTER JOIN (
    SELECT ....
    FROM TABLE
    JOIN TABLE ON ...
    JOIN TABLE ON ...
    JOIN TABLE ON ...
    JOIN TABLE ON ...
    WHERE ....
) ON COL IN (x, b, d .. )
```

Figure 1.2: Query approach.

enterprise data model may need to change, and Extract, Transform, Load (ETL) code needs to be re-generated or corrected. Sometimes the engineer who wrote the ETL code is not available anymore so another engineer needs to reverse engineer the code.

The overall issue is trust. During the 6 months (or 12, or 18, ...) which the data warehouse was being built, the data analyst continued to do their work through the previous *ad hoc* Spreadsheet and Query approaches. Even though those approaches are *ad hoc*, the data analyst trusts those answers because they themselves are in control. When the data analyst compares the answers to the same question between the *ad hoc* process they control and the data warehouse that they do not control, the answers are most probably going to be different. Guess which process is going to be trusted? This is why data warehouses fail: not for technical reasons but for *social reasons*, because they are not trusted.

Open questions include.

- How do we know what the data model actually means?

- Can we explain where each piece of data is coming from?

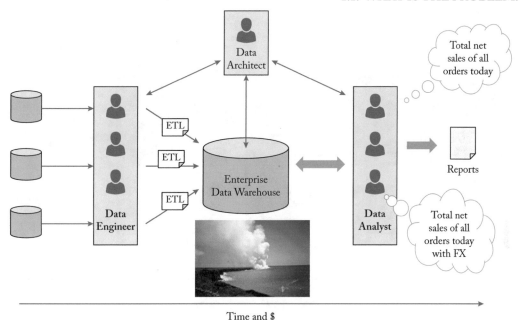

Figure 1.3: Data warehouse approach.

1.1.4 DATA LAKE APPROACH

A Data Lake is basically a Data Warehouse that (1) allows you to dump any type of data into it (a data warehouse only consists of structured/relational data) and (2) transformations are done after the data is in the lake: extract, load, and *then* transform (ELT) (Figure 1.4).

It is faster to load and centralize the data in one place. It is paramount to understand, however, that even if the data is physically co-located, it doesn't mean that the data has been integrated in any way. Every transformation is done independently. The open questions for the data warehouse scenario hold for data lakes too.

1.1.5 DATA WRANGLING APPROACH

A main drawback of the Data Warehouse and Data Lake approaches is that they depend too much on IT, who now becomes the bottleneck. Following the rise of self-service analytics tools, we are now encountering self-service *data wrangling tools* that enable data analysts to prepare the data with minimal assistance or intervention from IT (Figure 1.5).

The situation we encounter is that each data analyst can be wrangling the data in different ways, without communicating with other analysts. The process of wrangling the data is not just about cleaning data but also transforming the data to align with (some) business meaning. For example, each data analyst may be tasked to do different revenue projects, but they may each be

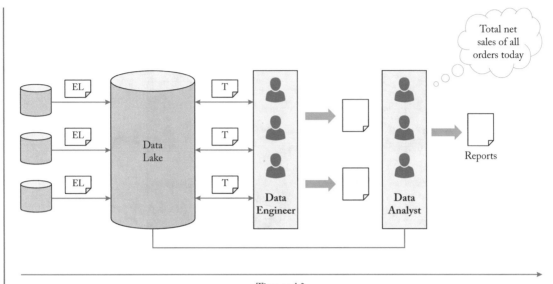

Figure 1.4: Data Lake approach.

transforming the data according to different definitions of revenue. In other words, each data analyst may be providing a different meaning (i.e., semantics) for the data.

This time, our open questions are

- How do we know that data wrangling is consistent across different data analysts?

- How do we know that data analysts are not "reinventing the wheel" and redoing work that should and could be reused?

1.1.6   SO WHAT?

We have observed a number of issues with existing approaches: First and foremost, there is a gap between the data and the meaning of the data, and our thesis is that if we do not bridge this gap we easily end up with systems that can be characterized as "garbage in, garbage out" (Figure 1.6).

A lot of work is being done over and over, there are tendencies to "boil the ocean," and data and knowledge work can easily be lost.

Gartner states that "Self-service analytics is often characterized by [. . .] an underlying data model that has been simplified or scaled down for ease of understanding and straightfor-ward data access."[6] This may be wishful thinking, but the fact remains that in a data-centric

---

[6]https://www.gartner.com/en/information-technology/glossary/self-service-analytics

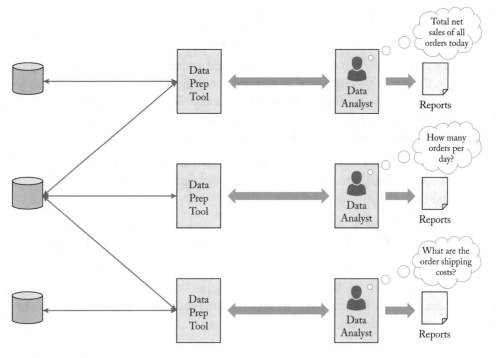

Figure 1.5: **Data Wrangling** approach.

Figure 1.6: **So What?**

architecture a single, simple, and extensible data model is exactly what we need [McComb, 2019].

Luckily, this is precisely what can be achieved with knowledge graphs.

1.2   KNOWLEDGE GRAPHS

1.2.1   WHAT IS A KNOWLEDGE GRAPH?

A *knowledge graph* represents a collection of real-world concepts (i.e., nodes) and relationships (i.e., edges) in the form of a graph used to link and integrate data coming from diverse sources. Knowledge graphs can be considered to achieve an early vision in computing, of creating intelligent systems that integrate knowledge and data on a large scale. In its simplest form, a knowledge graph encodes meaning and data together in the form of a graph:

- Knowledge (i.e., meaning): Concepts and the relationships between the concepts are first class citizens, meaning that it encodes knowledge of how the domain users understand the world.

- Graph (i.e., data): A data structure based on nodes and edges that enables integrating data coming from hetergeneous data sources, from unstructured to structured.

The popularity of the term "knowledge graph" stems from the announcement of the Google Knowledge Graph in 2012.[7] Since then, a plethora of small-, medium-, and large-scale companies have deployed knowledge graphs to enhance search, do recommendations, perform analytics and machine learning, etc.

1.2.2   WHY KNOWLEDGE GRAPHS?

Knowledge graphs provide a meaningful and reliable view of your enterprise data. We focus on two primary reasons:

Knowledge graphs bridge the data-meaning gap: This is accomplished by connecting the data consumers' business terminology with data, and enabling access of the data through this terminology. This means that data consumers and business users can access the data in their own terms which dramatically improves search, findability, clarity, accuracy, thus reducing the time and cost to identify accurate data to answer critical business questions. Furthermore, a knowledge graph can provide reasoning capabilities to infer new knowledge, thus allowing us to generate new insights and recommendations.

Knowledge graphs are a natural data model for data integration. The graph data model is flexible and nimble by nature, ideal for data integration. This implies that developers can quickly add and integrate data coming from a variety of sources. Furthermore, graphs enable tracking the lineage from the business concepts to the data, thus providing governance and explanability to the answers of the questions on the knowledge graph.

Let's break this down a bit more:

Knowledge graphs bridge the data-meaning gap between how business users understand the world and how the data is physically represented and stored in a database. Consider the

---

[7]https://blog.google/products/search/introducing-knowledge-graph-things-not/

domain of e-commerce. An order is placed by a customer. An order is shipped to an address. There may multiple addresses: a shipping address, a billing address, etc. An order has different order lines and an order line is connected to a product, and so forth. This is how a business users see the world of e-commerce. Very simple. However, the Order Management System's database does not store the data in that way. Ideally, the database schema would have a table called `Order` and a table called `Customer`, etc. Unfortunately, that is never the case in enterprise application databases, because the data is stored to benefit the application, not the data consumers. It is common that enterprise databases consist of thousands of tables with tens of thousands of attributes due to query workload requirements (vertical/horizontal partioning), custom fields (tables having hundreds of columns called `segment1`, `segment2`, etc.), and extending the application with new requirements often leads to the replication of data in a new table, in order to avoid altering a schema designed for a specific part of the application. This is known as the *application-centric quagmire* [McComb, 2018]. Thus, if a business user needs to access the data in the Order Management System, they would not understand it on their own, hence the data-meaning gap.

In a knowledge graph, the business terminology is represented as concepts and relationships. They can have different associated labels (synonyms), even in different languages. The concepts and relationships are connected with the underlying application databases through mappings. Business questions can be represented as queries in terms of the knowledge graph instead of the inscrutable application database schemas.

Knowledge graphs are a natural data model that makes data integration easier.

First, graphs are an ideal abstraction model. You can have different types of data sources such as relational databases as well as files in formats such as csv, xls, xml, json, text, etc. You can represent all these different data models in a graph.[8] Those thousands of tables of an order management system database can be represented in a single, simple knowledge graph about e-commerece. The output of Natural Language Processing (NLP) tasks such as entity extraction, relationship extraction, all feed the graph. Therefore, graphs are a common, unifying model for different models and formats of source data.

Second, graphs are flexible by nature. In a relational database you need to define the schema up front before you can load data. If you have to make changes to the schema, it can become a headache because you may need to restructure the way the data is modeled. However, when you work with a graph, all you add are more nodes and edges.

Finally, graphs enable integration. Consider two disparate graphs. How do you connect them? Just add edges between nodes. Therefore, integrating data in the form of graph boils down to creating relationships between the concepts.

Knowledge graphs are also gaining traction in a variety of use cases such as "Customer 360," identity graph, master data management, fraud detection, recommendation engines, social

---

[8]Recall that the focus of this book is on representing relational databases as knowledge graphs, but the fundamental ideas are more general.

networking, network operations, life science and drug discovery, among others. With a knowledge graph, organizations have the ability to execute graph analytics and algorithms (inferences, page rank, shortest path, etc.) that extend the capabilities of the state of the art.

1.2.3   WHY NOW?

Graph databases are hot. There are a plethora of companies whose products or services are either graph databases or functionality closely associated with graph databases.[9] The market is still nascent at the time of writing, but many mature products and services are already available and are used in production systems.

The W3C graph standards (RDF, SPARQL, etc.) have been around for two decades and at this point can be considered quite mature. The standards for property graphs are being developed, and the divide between the two families of graphs is getting smaller.

The tech giants have been adopting knowledge graphs [Noy et al., 2019]. In addition, there are numerous startups with products and services that were easier and faster to build and bring to market, thanks to graph databases and other graph technologies.

1.3   BACKGROUND

Before we get into the details of building knowledge graphs, let us discuss more generally the aforementioned problem of how to represent information about the real world.

1.3.1   HISTORY OF KNOWLEDGE GRAPHS

Graphs, as a branch of mathematics, date back at least to the 18th century and the German mathematician Leonhard Euler who posed a famous problem dubbed "Bridges of Königsberg" which now is in some ways considered the genesis of graph theory [Euler, 1736]. You could also argue that much of classical computer science is grounded in graphs and graph-based algorithms.

Theory aside, graphs—constructs consisting of nodes (also called "vertices") and edges—are a very intuitive and natural way to model information and as such are a good choice for us as a mechanism to represent the world. Knowledge graphs are the modern embodiment of one of the oldest subfields of artificial intelligence called *knowledge representation* (KR). The goal of KR is to facilitate the representation of information in such a way that automated systems can better interpret that information. To quote Brachman and Levesque [1985]:

> *The notion of representation of knowledge is at heart an easy one to understand. It simply has to do with writing down, in some language or communicative medium, descriptions or pictures that correspond in some salient way to the world or the state of the world. In Artificial Intel-*

---

[9]That includes the employers of both authors of this book.

> *ligence (AI), we are concerned with writing down descriptions of the world in such a way that an intelligent machine can come to new conclusions about its environment by formally manipulating these descriptions.*

This characterization is relevant, since we will look at KR from the viewpoint of facilitating not only the management of representations, but also making such representations actionable. This should be seen in the context of what [Fikes and Kehler, 1985] define as the basic criteria for a knowledge representation language, namely *expressive power* (measuring the possibility and ease of expressing different pieces of knowledge), *understandability* (measuring whether knowledge can be understood by humans) and *accessibility* (measuring how effectively the knowledge can be accessed and used). Also, one of the key realizations about KR is that not all formalisms or structures qualify as representation; instead, a representation formalism needs to be associated with a *semantic theory* to provide the basis for reasoning [Hayes, 1974] and the means to define its meaning.

The early work on KR (in the 1960s) focused on human associative memory—mostly in a metaphoric sense—and introduced associative formalisms and structures for capturing information about the world. These structures, known as semantic networks [Brachman, 1979, Quillian, 1967, Woods, 1975], represent information as labeled graphs where nodes denote concepts and edges denote relationships between concepts. Modern knowledge graphs are not far at all from this original idea.

Semantic networks were criticised for their weak formal foundations, and attempts to mitigate this led to the introduction of frames, another approach to KR [Fikes and Kehler, 1985, Karp, 1992, Minsky, 1975]. The simplistic view of frame-based representation is that a frame represents an object or a concept. Attached to the frame is a collection of properties, and these may initially be filled with default values. It is easy to think of frames as a collection of linked objects that form a (knowledge) graph, and indeed frames paved the way for logic- and graph-based KR and modern knowledge graphs.

Subsequent work on logic, particularly the push to find tractable subsets of first-order predicate calculus, has given rise to description logics, logic-based formalizations of object-oriented modeling, and languages such as OWL.

For further details on the history of knowledge graphs, we refer the reader to Gutierrez and Sequeda [2021].[10]

1.3.2   SEMANTICS

The term "semantics" is much overused and abused in today's information systems vernacular. What, exactly, does this term mean? In the context of information systems, semantics defines how data "behaves" and how machines can interpret data, and when properly applied, can free

---

[10]See also: http://knowledgegraph.today/.

us from having to "hard-wire" logic into software systems and application code. In that sense, it gives rise to "data-driven" processing. But where does semantics come from? In very pragmatic terms, it is embodied in the following:

1. relationships between data (e.g., USD) and definitions of data (e.g., currency);

2. relationships within data (e.g., 10 and USD); and

3. hard-wired in software (e.g., calculation of net sales).

The first two categories allow us to move toward data-driven processing, something where (most of) the logic of a system is embodied in the data and the definitions of data, and the software itself acts as an "interpreter" of the data and its definitions. This is drastically different from category #3 above. Most of today's information systems still belong in this last category, unfortunately, forcing software work, upgrades, new versions, etc., whenever we want to make changes to processing logic.

Separating domain-specific processing logic from software code and rather associating this with data, whether by reference or by carrying these definitions with the data itself, also improves interoperability in data interchange, especially when data is being exchanged between different organizations.

1.3.3   SEMANTIC WEB

The Semantic Web [Berners-Lee et al., 2001] is a vision that was introduced in the late 1990s and early 2000s, motivated by the needs to enable better integration and "operationalization" of data on the Web. The idea is basically predicated on giving data accessible formal semantics, and allowing the definitions of semantics to be exchanged together with the actual data. The World Wide Web Consortium (W3C, an organization that manages many of the technical specifications of the Web) produced a set of standards for the Semantic Web, and by doing so laid the groundwork for modern knowledge graphs. The term "Web" in Semantic Web refers to the fact that, in effect, the whole vision is about building support for KR and graphs using web technologies, and thus the Semantic Web does not imply that by using these technologies you have to put your data "out there" on the public web (albeit that also is possible as we will demonstrate later). Foundational Web technologies (such as HTTP or URIs) are well understood and widely supported, making them an ideal foundation for building distributed KR systems.

The Semantic Web is predicated on a few overarching principles: make data accessible, give it accessible semantics (i.e., definitions of data in the form of ontologies, something we will address in the next section), and—optionally—provide mechanisms for reasoning about data (again, with the help of ontologies).

1.3.4 MODELS, ONTOLOGIES, AND SCHEMATA

At the heart of representing information is the notion of a model, a definition of how your data is structured and what it means—its semantics, that is. Typically, a model defines both the physical and the logical structure of information, but in this book we will show that *mappings* allow us to build knowledge graphs by focusing on logical modeling, as the physical aspects have been "taken care of." A modeling language provides the means to define a model and the semantics of data that conforms to the model. In KR, this model is often called an *ontology*, as already mentioned; it is called that because of its relationship with metaphysics: we define what is in the "world," its various concepts and objects, look like and how they behave. In this book, rather than using the term ontology (and taking on all the nuances and implications of the term), we will call our models "knowledge graphs schemas" [11] instead, and these will run the gamut from simple notions of logically structuring your data to potentially complex semantic definitions and constraints.

1.4 WHY THIS BOOK?

This book is about designing and building knowledge graphs from relational databases. To introduce the landscape, let us briefly look at the main practical challenges of knowledge graph design and construction.

First, we must engage in domain modeling or "ontology engineering," in the creation and definition of a sufficiently broad and shared data model: the knowledge graph schema [Kendall and McGuinness, 2019, Tudorache, 2020]. Second, we must do "mapping engineering," namely to understand how existing (non-graph) data sources are mapped or transformed for the purposes of creating the eventual knowledge graph.

Engineering a knowledge graph schema is difficult in and of itself. The field—earlier often referred to as "knowledge acquisition"—was prolific throughout the 1990s. Early seminal work includes Fox and Grüninger [1997], Uschold and King [1995], followed by a multitude of methodologies, notably METHONTOLOGY [Fernández-López et al., 1997]. For an early survey, see Corcho et al. [2003]. Research in this field continues to progress by focusing on the sophisticated use of competency questions [Azzaoui et al., 2013, Ren et al., 2014], test-driven development [Keet and Lawrynowicz, 2016], ontology design patterns [Hitzler et al., 2016], reuse [Suárez-Figueroa et al., 2012], etc., just to name a few. Furthermore, numerous knowledge graph schemas have been designed with reuse in mind, such as the Finance Industry

---

[11]We are aware that the correct plural form of "schema" is, in fact, "schemata," and yet we have decided to say "schemas" in this book because of the prevalence of the incorrect form in our industry. Our apologies for this. It seems that this is yet another English term molested by computer scientists ("indexes," instead of the correct form "indices," is another one that comes to mind).

Business Ontology (FIBO),[12] Gist[13] for general business concepts, Schema.org,[14] etc. We will dive into reusing external knowledge graph schemas in Section 2.2.3.

It seems to be a fair conjecture that knowledge graph schema engineering should actually not be that much of a challenge. This would be the case if the ultimate deliverable was just a schema in isolation. However, populating a knowledge graph schema with data seems to be an afterthought and not a key component of existing schema engineering methodologies. In the context of designing a knowledge graph, both the schema and the mappings that generate the data sourced from relational databases must be first-class citizens.

Let's assume that a knowledge graph schema has either been created via an established methodology or an existing schema is being reused. The next step is to map relational databases and other data sources to the schema in order to generate the knowledge graph. One common practice bootstraps the process with a direct mapping that generates a so-called putative knowledge graph schema from the database schema [Sequeda et al., 2012]. This practice suggests approaching the problem as an schema-matching problem between the source putative knowledge graph schema and the target knowledge graph schema. In theory, this can work [Jiménez-Ruiz et al., 2015], but per our experience, this has not yet become (and may never become) practical in the real-world for the following reasons.

- As previously discussed, enterprise database schemas are very large, consisting of thousands of tables and tens of thousands of attributes. Schema developers frequently and notoriously use acronyms and peculiar abbreviations for tables and columns (i.e., they use virtually meaningless names). Some commercial systems make frequent use of numbered columns for enterprise-specific data with no explicit semantic meaning whatsoever stored in the database (e.g., segment1, segment2). The data stored in these columns may also consist of codes that are meaningless by themselves.

- Simple one-to-one schema correspondences are rare. We have found throughout our real-world experience that complex mappings dominate. That is, a mapping often integrates calculations and needs to incorporate business logic rules while simultaneously considering many database values. For example, the notion of "net sales of an order" is defined as "gross sales minus taxes and discounts given." The tax rate can be different depending on location, and the discount can depend on the type of customer. A business user needs to provide these definitions before mappings can be created. Thus, without clairvoyance, automating the mappings is often simply not feasible.

Early on in our practice we observed that schemas and mappings must be developed holistically. That is, there is a continual back-and-forth between schema and mapping engineering. Furthermore, this process is a team effort. For these reasons, we argue that schema engineering

---

[12]https://spec.edmcouncil.org/fibo/
[13]http://semanticarts.com/gist
[14]https://schema.org/

methodologies must be extended to support how the schema should be populated via mappings in order to build a knowledge graph in conjunction with a team consisting of data producers, data consumers, and knowledge scientist.

CHAPTER 2

Designing Enterprise Knowledge Graphs

The architecture to build an enterprise knowledge graph from relational databases consists of three definitional entities.

- The source relational database: this is where the data is stored and is physically structured following a relational schema for which data producers are responsible.

- The target knowledge graph: this is a conceptual model of the domain, represented in a graph, which uses the *lingua franca* of the data consumers.

- The mappings: declarative associations between select contents of the source relational database schema and the target knowledge graph schema.

With these three components in place, business questions can be defined in terms of the knowledge graph schema's conceptual abstraction instead of the individual heterogeneous source databases' physical structures. Systems that implement knowledge graphs can be realized in a physical or virtual way. Finally, the resulting knowledge graph is used by business users and systems to access the knowledge and data.

2.1 SOURCE: RELATIONAL DATABASES

Relational databases have been at the forefront of enterprise data management since the 1980s, after the creation of the relational model by Codd in the 1970s [Codd, 1970].

These databases model data with *tables* and *columns*. A key characteristic of relational databases is to maintain consistency of the data using integrity constraints such as *primary key* and *foreign keys*. The rows in a table are the data values, and there is a standard query language: SQL.

2.2 TARGET: KNOWLEDGE GRAPH

A *knowledge graph*, as the name implies, represents knowledge and data in the form of a graph. As discussed in the previous chapter, the main elements of a graph are *nodes* and *edges*. The nodes represent concepts such as Customer, Order, Product, Address, etc., and the things that

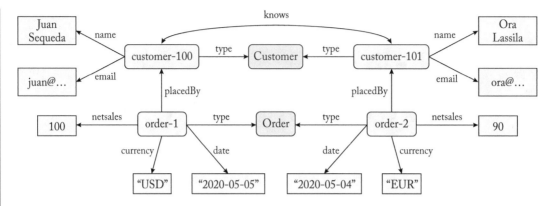

Figure 2.1: Graph.

instantiate them (in our examples: customer-1, order-1, etc.). The edges represent relationships between nodes, such as "Order" "placed by" "Customer" and "order-1" "placed by" "customer-1."

There are two prevalent graph models: RDF Graphs and Property Graphs.

2.2.1   RDF GRAPH

The RDF (Resource Description Framework) graph model is a directed edge-labeled graph. It consists of a set of nodes and a set of directed labeled edges between these nodes. RDF is a standardized data model recommended by the W3C, and has been around since the late 1990s. It is also the basic building block of the Semantic Web [Berners-Lee et al., 2001].

The grouping *node-edge-node* is known as an RDF "triple." The head node is called the *subject*, the edge is called the *predicate*, and the tail node is called the *object*. A set of RDF triples is called an *RDF graph*. Given that RDF was designed within the context of the World Wide Web, it uses IRIs (Internationalized Resource Identifiers) as a means to identify nodes and edges. For a given triple, the subject must either be an IRI (an "IRI reference" is the term the RDF specifications use) or a "blank node" (this is essentially a node that only has an internal identity and cannot be addressed directly in a query, but we will ignore those in this book). The predicate must always be an IRI—there are no unidentified or "unlabeled" edges in RDF. The object can be an IRI, a blank node, or a "literal value" such as a string or a number.

Example 2.1
Consider the graph in Figure 2.1.

The graph in Figure 2.1 can be represented as an RDF graph by separating each RDF triple, as shown in Table 2.1 (for clarity, we have used simple identifiers instead of full IRIs).

Table 2.1: Table with separated each RDF triple

Subject	Predicate	Object
customer-100	type	Customer
customer-100	name	"Juan Sequeda"
customer-100	email	"juan@data.world"
customer-100	knows	customer-101
customer-101	type	Customer
customer-100	name	"Ora Lasilla"
customer-101	email	"ora@amazon.com"
customer-101	knows	customer-100
order-1	type	Order
order-1	netsales	"100"
order-1	currency	"USD"
order-1	orderdate	"2021-01-01"
order-1	placedBy	customer-100
order-2	type	Order
order-2	netsales	"90"
order-1	currency	"EUR"
order-2	orderdate	"2021-01-02"
order-2	placedBy	customer-102

2.2.2   PROPERTY GRAPH

The Property Graph model provides additional flexibility (or complexity, depending on how you look at it) when compared to directed edge labeled graphs, by allowing a set of property-value pairs and a label to be associated with the nodes and edges in a graph. Said in another way, Property Graph nodes and edges are *structured objects*, as opposed to RDF where they are just identifiers and have no structure. As of 2021, Property Graphs are in the process of standardization by ISO. They are used in graph databases such as Neo4j and Tigergraph. Some graph databases, such as Amazon Neptune, allow the use of either Property Graphs or RDF. Current, pre-standardization property graphs lack some of the "web-friendly" features of RDF, such as global identifiers (IRIs) for nodes and edge labels. This can complicate use cases where interoperability and information exchange is needed, as the implementation now requires one to "re-invent" those features.

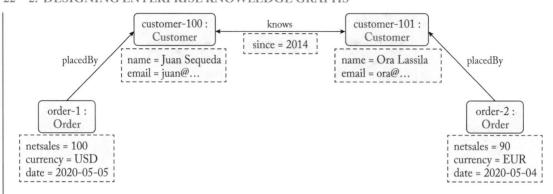

Figure 2.2: Property Graph.

Example 2.2
The RDF Graph shown in Example 2.1 can be visually represented as a Property Graph as in Figure 2.2.

This example is extended by adding the property-value pair *since=2014* to the edge knows. This really is the fundamental difference between Property Graphs and RDF. At the time of writing, W3C is working on a new RDF specification, called RDF-star (or RDF*), that allows similar modeling in RDF as well.[1]

2.2.3   KNOWLEDGE GRAPH SCHEMA

A knowledge graph schema is a definition that provides organization to the knowledge graph data, represented in a formal language.

In the RDF Graph model, the Knowledge Graph Schema is known as an *ontology* and it is represented in the RDF Schema (RDFS) or OWL (Web Ontology Language) languages [Uschold, 2018].[2] There are three main components.

- **Class**: is an abstraction mechanism for creating a collection of objects with similar characteristics. These objects are called *instances* of a class. For example, a class can be "Customer" and "customer-100," "customer-101" are instances of this class. A class and instances are nodes in the knowledge graph.

- **Datatype Property**: these are relationships between instances of classes (the *domain*) and literals (the *range*). For example, "name" is a datatype property that relates all the instances of the Customer class to a string datatype. Customer is the domain of the name datatype property while string is the range. A datatype property is an edge in the

---

[1]https://w3c.github.io/rdf-star/
[2]For all intents and purposes, you can think of RDFS as a simple schema language, and OWL as an extension of RDFS that provides more expressive power.

knowledge graph from an instance node to a data value. For example, "customer-100" "name" "Juan Sequeda."

- **Object Property**: these are relationships between instances of two classes. For example, "placedBy" is an object property that relates all the instances of the "Order" class to instances of the "Customer" class. "Order" is the domain and "Customer" is the range. An object property is an edge in the knowledge graph between two instance nodes. For example, "order-1" "placedBy" "customer-100."

Finally, a class may be a **subclass** of another, thus inheriting the properties from its parent superclass. This corresponds to logical subsumption. In Section 4.3.2, we briefly discuss how subclass can be used for reasoning.

The Property Graph model does not yet have an agreed upon schema language. As of 2021, the LDBC Property Graph Schema Working Group is in the process of defining recommendations of schema languages for Property Graphs.

External Knowledge Graph Schema

Knowledge graph schemas, namely ontologies, are a means of not just representing knowledge but also sharing knowledge. The Semantic Web community, specifically the ontology engineering community, has developed methodologies to build knowledge graph schemas that can be reused (see Section 1.4). Industry-specific communities have followed these best practices and built reusable knowledge graph schemas. Therefore, instead of creating a schema from scratch, you can reuse existing schemas. However, you don't have to reuse them as-is. You can take parts of an existing schema—and possibly extend it—when designing a schema that satisfies your organization's needs. RDFS and OWL were designed for extensibility. Finally, the source relational databases still need to be mapped to the knowledge graph schema, regardless of whether this schema was created or reused.

If different organizations reuse the same schema for their knowledge graphs, they can easily exchange data that has a shared meaning. This applies both between different parts of a single enterprise as well as across enterprises. A successful example is https://schema.org/, which is a shared vocabulary that makes it easier for any webmasters to annotate their webpages in a way that they can be processed by any applications crawling the web.

Over the past decade, many reusable knowledge graph schemas in various industries have been created. A non-exhaustive list:

- Life Science: https://bioportal.bioontology.org/

- Finance: https://spec.edmcouncil.org/fibo/

- Oil and Gas: https://www.iso.org/standard/70694.html

- Healthcare: https://www.hl7.org/fhir/

- Real Estate: https://w3id.org/rec/full/

- Social Network: http://xmlns.com/foaf/spec/

- Cultural Heritage: https://pro.europeana.eu/page/edm-documentation

- General Business Concepts: https://www.semanticarts.com/gist/

- Metadata: https://www.dublincore.org/schemas/rdfs/, https://open-kos.org, https://www.w3.org/TR/vocab-dcat-2/

- Provenance: https://www.w3.org/TR/prov-o/

2.2.4 AN ABSTRACT GRAPH NOTATION USED IN THIS BOOK

The goal of this book is to provide the elements to design and build knowledge graphs, regardless of the underlying graph model. We therefore use an abstract notation and terminology that is a generalization over RDF graphs and Property Graphs. The main elements are: Concepts, Concept Attributes, Relationships, and Relationship Attributes.

- **Concept:** a node in the graph that represents a real-world entity. For example

    (Customer)
    (Order)

    An instance of a Concept is also a node in a graph. The instance is connected to the Concept through a special relationship called $-$type$\rightarrow$. For example: order-1 and order-2 are instances of the Order concept, and customer-100 and customer-101 are instances of the Customer concept:

    (order-1) $-$type$\rightarrow$ (Order)
    (order-2) $-$type$\rightarrow$ (Order)
    (customer-100) $-$type$\rightarrow$ (Customer)
    (customer-101) $-$type$\rightarrow$ (Customer)

- **Relationship**: the edge in a graph that represents a connection between two concepts. For example:

    (Order) $-$placedBy$\rightarrow$ (Customer)
    (Customer) $-$knows$\rightarrow$ (Customer)

    The relationship in a graph represents connections between instances of concepts. For example, order-1 is placedBy customer-100, order-2 is placedBy customer-101, and customer-100 knows customer-101:

$$(\text{order-1}) - \text{placedBy} \rightarrow (\text{customer-100})$$
$$(\text{order-2}) - \text{placedBy} \rightarrow (\text{customer-101})$$
$$(\text{customer-100}) - \text{knows} \rightarrow (\text{customer-101})$$

- **Concept Attribute**: represents a means of associating data values to a concept. It is represented as an edge in a graph that represents a connection between a concept and a data type. For example:

$$(\text{Customer}) - \text{name} \rightarrow [\text{string}]$$

The concept attribute connects an instance of a concept with a data value. For example, "name = Juan Sequeda" is an attribute associated with customer-100 and "name = Ora Lassila" is an attribute associated with customer-101:

$$(\text{customer-100}) - \text{name} \rightarrow [\text{JuanSequeda}]$$
$$(\text{customer-101}) - \text{name} \rightarrow [\text{OraLassila}]$$

- **Relationship Attribute**: represents a means of associating data values to a relationship. It is represented as a key-value pair associated with a relationship where the key is an attribute and the value is a datatype

$$(\text{Customer}) - \text{knows}[\text{since} = \text{date}] \rightarrow (\text{Customer})$$

For example, "since = 2004" is an attribute associated with the relationships knows:

$$(\text{customer-100}) - \text{knows}[\text{since} = 2014] \rightarrow (\text{customer-101})$$

Note that we are providing simple identifiers for the nodes and edges: (Customer), (Order), (order-1), (customer-1), −placedBy→, −name→, −knows[since =]→. See Section 2.2.6 for more information on identifiers.

This abstract graph model can be related to both RDF Graphs and Property Graphs. In RDF, a concept is called Class, a concept attribute is called Datatype Property, and a relationship is called Object Property. Relationship attributes in RDF are a bit trickier (this, in fact, is the primary difference between RDF graphs and Property Graphs). In "plain" RDF, edges cannot have attributes, but this can be addressed in a couple of different ways, either by changing how one models relationships, or via a mechanism called "reification" which the RDF standard supports.[3]

In Property Graphs [Bonifati et al., 2018], a concept is a node that has a label which is a descriptive identifier of the real-world entity it represents. Concept attributes are key-value pairs,

---

[3] See a note in the previous section about the emerging W3C RDF-star specification which addresses this issue.

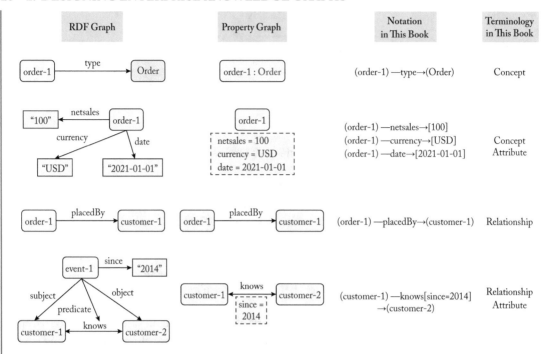

Figure 2.3: Comparing RDF and Property Graphs and the notation and terminology used in this book.

or so called properties, associated with a node that provides the actual data an object represents. Relationships are edges between the nodes that also have labels. Relationship attributes are key-value pairs associated with the edges (Figure 2.3).

2.2.5   GRAPH QUERY LANGUAGES

The RDF and Property Graph models have their own types of query languages. SPARQL (aka "SPARQL Protocol and RDF Query Language") is the standardized query language for RDF.

As of 2021, ISO is in the process of standardizing a query language for Property Graphs: GQL. There are a variety of open and proprietary property graph query languages: Neo4j's Cypher, TigerGraph's GSQL, Oracle's PGQL, Apache Gremlin, and G-CORE.

We will not focus on query languages because the focus of this book is in the design and building of knowledge graphs and not querying knowledge graphs.

2.2.6   IDENTIFIERS

Metcalfe's Law shows that the value of a network is proportional to the square of the number of nodes in the network. This law can be applied to data (albeit not directly with the proportions).

A knowledge graph's value increases when it is the result of integrating multiple disparate data sources [Hendler and Golbeck, 2008].

To accelerate the integration of data, it is beneficial to have an agreed upon *identitier* mechanism or convention. An identifier is a label that globally and uniquely identifies an element in a knowledge graph.[4] Consider building a knowledge graph that integrates data from an order management system (OMS) and a customer relationship management (CRM) system. The order management system will have data about customers and the orders they have purchased, while the CRM system will have more detailed data about the customers. By agreeing on the identifier scheme for a customer, once a knowledge graph for the OMS and the CRM are created, all the customer data is integrated because they are referring to the same thing (e.g., the same customer customer-100). It is important to note that the identifier must uniquely identify an element not just within the database it comes from, but also be globally unique with respect to all the databases that are being integrated, and even for future databases. Namespaces can be used to create global unique identifiers. Effectively, identifiers serve a global join keys that can overcome the physical barriers of database applications within your organization.

Furthermore, identifiers should also be applied to the knowledge graph schema: Concepts (Order, Customer), Attributes (currency, name), and Relationships (placedBy, knows). This provides a mechanism for reuse and interoperability of the schema with a clear meaning (i.e., if we are referring to the same thing, we know what we are talking about) that enables a shared understanding of the data, democratizes the access to the data, and thus increases the use of the data.

The best identifiers are SIMPLE.[a] The following is a guide to design global and universal identifiers:

- **S**torable: You should be able to store the identifier offline. For instance, order ID may be stored in an OMS and ERP systems.

- **I**mmutable: It should not change over time. An order ID is usually the same within an organization.

- **M**eticulous: The same entity in two different systems should resolve to the same ID. It should be very difficult (or impossible) for two occurrences of the same order to claim they have a different order IDs.

- **P**ortable: An order ID can be moved from one system to another.

- **L**ow-cost: The ID needs to be cheap (or even free). If it is too expensive, the transaction costs will make it hard to use in many situations.

---

[4]In this book we use examples with identifiers that obviously are not globally unique: For example, order-1 is an identifier for the instance of Order while customer-100 is an identifier for the instance of Customer. This is done so that we can keep our examples terse.

- **E**stablished: It needs to cover almost all of its subjects. An order ID covers all the orders.

[a]https://www.safegraph.com/blog/data-standards-and-the-join-key

Therefore, an important initial step in designing a knowledge graph is to decide on an appropriate identifier scheme for the knowledge graph schema and the data elements. Even though conventions may evolve over time, investing upfront thought on identifiers is crucial. Identifiers are the glue that connects data sources together and effectively establishes the graph.

An important and related topic to identifiers is entity resolution which is the task of finding records in different datasets that refer to the same entity. We briefly touch on this topic in Section 4.3.2. However, entity resolution deserves its own deep dive which is out of scope for this book.

Identifiers in RDF Graphs

The notion of identifiers is built into the RDF model through Internationalized Resource Identifiers (IRI). An IRI is an internet protocol standard which builds on the Uniform Resource Identifiers (URI) by permitting not just the ASCII character set but also Universal Character Set characters such as Chinese, Japanese, etc. IRIs are part of the architecture of the World Wide Web[5] and follow the principle: *Global naming leads to global network effects.* By design, IRIs have global scope. Thus, two different appearances of an IRI denote the same thing.

That is why the subjects, predicates, and objects of an RDF triple are IRIs. In an RDF knowledge graph, the schema elements are identified by IRIs. The identifier for the concept Order in a RDF knowledge graph schema could be:

    https://schema.org/Order

The identifier for the attribute name could be:

    https://schema.org/name

The identifier for the relationship paymentMethod could be:

    https://schema.org/paymentMethod

These IRIs can be made dereferencable, meaning that you can even look them up on your browser (via HTTP GET).

As we mentioned earlier, the instances in an RDF knowledge graph are also identified using IRIs. The real identifier for the `order-1`—which is an instance of an `Order`—could be:

    https://mycompany.com/data/order-1

[5]https://www.w3.org/TR/webarch/#identification

Instead of writing these (possibly) long IRIs, one can create shortcuts by defining a prefix. For example, the prefix `schema` can be name for `https://schema.org/`, therefore `schema:Order` is equivalent to `https://schema.org/Order`.

Establishing Identifiers from Relational Data

In order to dynamically establish identifiers from relational data, we need to define an identifier template. This is a format string that can be used to build identifier strings from multiple components. An identifier template references columns of a relational table. Our notation is to enclose column names in curly braces ("{" and "}"): template-{ID}

Common practice is to use a column that is a key (primary or unique) of a table. However, a key is locally unique to the table. Consider a table that has a column id which is the primary key. A row may have the value 1 as the id and therefore uniquely identifies that row in the table. However, the value 1 may also appear as a primary key column for another table. In order to make the identifier globally unique, we need to combine the key column with some identifying string.

Example 2.3

Consider the table `order` that has a primary key column `oid` and a table `customer` with a primary key column `cid`. Each of these tables have a row where oid and cid are both the value 1. In order to make a globally unique identifier, one could define the identifier template for customer as customer-{cid} and the identifier template for order as order-{oid}. The result of applying the template to the relational data will result in (customer-1) and (order-1).

As mentioned earlier, in this book we use simple identifiers for the sake of easier readability. In other words, we do not pretend that (customer-1) would be globally unique. For RDF Knowledge Graphs, we could change the prefix `customer-` to something that makes the identifier a valid IRI would make the resulting identifiers globally unique (e.g., the prefix could be `https://mycompany.com/data/customer-` instead).

2.2.7   MODELING

Modeling can be considered an art and a science. An art because beauty (or in this case, a form of correctness) is in the eye of the beholder (a data consumer). For one user, a data model can be too general, for someone else, the same model could be too complicated, and for another user it could be just right. It is also a science because the model can have implications on technical factors, such as the resulting size of data, size of query, and query performance.

Consider modeling the following scenario: an Order has a shipping address. An address has a street number, street name, city, state, postal code, and country.

Scenario 1: Order and Address are Concepts

$$(Order) - hasShippingAddress \rightarrow (Address)$$

$$(\text{Address}) - \text{streetNumber} \rightarrow [\text{string}]$$
$$(\text{Address}) - \text{streetName} \rightarrow [\text{string}]$$
$$(\text{Address}) - \text{city} \rightarrow [\text{string}]$$
$$(\text{Address}) - \text{state} \rightarrow [\text{string}]$$
$$(\text{Address}) - \text{postalCode} \rightarrow [\text{string}]$$
$$(\text{Address}) - \text{country} \rightarrow [\text{string}]$$

Scenario 2: Order, Address, and Country are Concepts

$$(\text{Order}) - \text{hasShippingAddress} \rightarrow (\text{Address})$$
$$(\text{Address}) - \text{locatedIn} \rightarrow (\text{Country})$$
$$(\text{Address}) - \text{streetNumber} \rightarrow [\text{string}]$$
$$(\text{Address}) - \text{streetName} \rightarrow [\text{string}]$$
$$(\text{Address}) - \text{city} \rightarrow [\text{string}]$$
$$(\text{Address}) - \text{state} \rightarrow [\text{string}]$$
$$(\text{Address}) - \text{postalCode} \rightarrow [\text{string}]$$
$$(\text{Country}) - \text{countryName} \rightarrow [\text{string}]$$

Scenario 3: Order, Address, State, and Country are Concepts

$$(\text{Order}) - \text{hasShippingAddress} \rightarrow (\text{Address})$$
$$(\text{Address}) - \text{locatedIn} \rightarrow (\text{State})$$
$$(\text{State}) - \text{locatedIn} \rightarrow (\text{Country})$$
$$(\text{Address}) - \text{streetNumber} \rightarrow [\text{string}]$$
$$(\text{Address}) - \text{streetName} \rightarrow [\text{string}]$$
$$(\text{Address}) - \text{city} \rightarrow [\text{string}]$$
$$(\text{Address}) - \text{state} \rightarrow [\text{string}]$$
$$(\text{Address}) - \text{postalCode} \rightarrow [\text{string}]$$
$$(\text{State}) - \text{stateName} \rightarrow [\text{string}]$$
$$(\text{Country}) - \text{countryName} \rightarrow [\text{string}]$$

On one side, all address attributes (street number, name, city, state, etc.) are associated to an Address concept, as shown in Scenario 1. Attributes can be decomposed into their own concepts. Scenario 2 depicts Country being a standalone concept. Scenario 3 depicts State and Country being standalone concepts. We could continue decomposing (or normalize) these until we get to the most granular level: every attribute associated to the Address concept of Scenario 1 becomes its own standalone concept.

Which model is better? Which one is worse? This is a tricky question and the answer is: it depends. You have to decide how to balance between practicality and "purity" of the data model. A data consumer may think about the world in a very granular way (purity). The designer of the knowledge graph needs to think about the identifiers for each concept, the size of the graph, the complexity of the queries, and the performance implications (practicality).

A rule of thumb: if you have a need to uniquely identify a thing in order to point and reference it because you are going to add information about that thing, then make that thing a concept. Otherwise, keep that thing as an attribute associated with an existing concept.

For example, address, state, and country should be their own concepts because there can be clear identifiers for those things and information associated with them (abbreviations, population, etc.). What about post code? Maybe. What about Street name? Probably not (unless you have a geographic use case).

Graph modeling is important. The choices made matter to the data consumers and designers of the knowledge graph. Note that these questions are not unique to graphs. Actually, graphs by default are in the sixth normal form (6NF). These same considerations apply to relational data modeling and conceptual models in general.

We do not try to educate the reader about relational and graph modeling, but we do want to make sure they understand that they need to learn about modeling. Therefore, we refer the reader to Allemang et al. [2020] and Alexopoulos [2020]. Our book is in between those two: how to map from a relational model to a graph model.

2.3   MAPPINGS: RELATIONAL DATABASE TO KNOWLEDGE GRAPH

A mapping is a function that represents the relationship from a source data model to a target data model. Mappings are used to represent how a relational database (the source) can be represented in a Knowledge Graph (the target). Mappings are commonly represented in a declarative formalism such as a rule language. A rule is an IF <condition> THEN <conclusion> construct where the <condition> is known as the body of the rule (or antecedant) and <conclusion> is known as the head of the rule (or consequent). In a mapping, the body of the rule is a condition that corresponds to the source data model and the head of the rule is a conclusion corresponding to the target data model. A set of rules corresponds to a mapping. We use the following notation to represent a mapping rule:

Once mappings have been defined, they can then be applied in a materialization or virtualization approach. In a materialization approach, also known as ETL (Extract, Transforms, and Load), the mappings are used to physically transform the relational databases into a knowledge graph, which would then be loaded into a graph database. In other words, the mappings represents the transforms. Mappings correspond to the T (transformation) of ETL. In rule engine parlance, this approach is called *forward chaining*.

In a virtualization approach, the mappings are used to rewrite queries in terms of the Knowledge Graph (e.g., SPARQL, Cypher) into SQL queries over the relational databases. In rule engine parlance, this approach is called *backward chaining*. We will dive into these details in the tools section.

There are two types of mappings: Direct Mapping and Custom Mappings.

2.3.1   DIRECT MAPPING

A direct mapping is a default and automatic representation of a relational database as a knowledge graph, without any human intervention [Sequeda et al., 2012]. The resulting knowledge graph mirrors the relational database schema. A direct mapping consists of a set of fixed rules that are applied to all relational databases. If changes are to be made to the rules, then we would be defining a Custom Mapping (see the next section).

The definition of a Direct Mapping is the following.

- Table is a Concept: each table in the relational database represents a concept and each row in the table represents a node that is an instance of the concept.

- Column is a Concept Attribute: each column of a table is an attribute associated to the concept which has been directly mapped to the corresponding table.

- Foreign Key is a Relationship: each column that is a foreign key is a relationship going from the concept which has been directly mapped to the corresponding table and going to the concept which has been directly mapping to the referencing table.

- Primary Key(s) columns are using in the template to create an identifier for each row in a table.

Example 2.4

Consider the following relational database. The `sales_flat_order` table stores all the order transactions and `customer_entity` stores all the data about customers. The column `entity_id` is the primary key of the `sales_flat_order` table. The column `entity_id` is the primary key of the `customer_entity` table. The column `customer_id` of the `sales_flat_order` table is a foreign key that references the column `entity_id` of the `customer_entity` table.

sales_flat_order			
entity_id	grand_total	order_currency_code	customer_id
1	110	USD	100
2	100	EUR	101

customer_entity		
entity_id	email	is_active
100	juan@data.world	1
101	ora@amazon.com	1
102	alice@email.com	0

The resulting knowledge graph schema based on a direct mapping is the following:

```
(sales_flat_order)
(customer_entity)
(sales_flat_order) −sales_flat_order-customer_id→ (customer_entity)
(sales_flat_order) −entity_id→ [int]
(sales_flat_order) −grand_total→ [float]
(sales_flat_order) −order_currency_code→ [string]
(sales_flat_order) −customer_id→ [int]
(customer_entity) −entity_id→ [int]
(customer_entity) −email→ [string]
(customer_entity) −is_active→ [int]
```

The resulting knowledge graph based on the direct mapping is the following:

```
(sales_flat_order-1) −type→ (sales_flat_order)
(sales_flat_order-1) −entity_id→ [1]
(sales_flat_order-1) −grand_total→ [100]
(sales_flat_order-1) −order_currency_code→ [USD]
(sales_flat_order-1) −customer_id→ [100]
(sales_flat_order-1) −sales_flat_order-customer_id→ (customer_entity-100)
(sales_flat_order-2) −type→ (sales_flat_order)
(sales_flat_order-2) −entity_id→ [2]
(sales_flat_order-2) −grand_total→ [100]
(sales_flat_order-2) −order_currency_code→ [EUR]
(sales_flat_order-2) −customer_id→ [102]
(sales_flat_order-2) −sales_flat_order-customer_id→ (customer_entity-102)
(customer_entity-100) −type→ (customer_entity)
(customer_entity-100) −entity_id→ [100]
(customer_entity-100) −email→ [juan@data.world]
(customer_entity-100) −is_active→ [1]
(customer_entity-101) −type→ (customer_entity)
(customer_entity-101) −entity_id→ [101]
(customer_entity-101) −email→ [ora@amazon.com]
(customer_entity-101) −is_active→ [1]
(customer_entity-102) −type→ (customer_entity)
(customer_entity-102) −entity_id→ [102]
(customer_entity-102) −email→ [alice@email.com]
(customer_entity-102) −is_active→ [0]
```

If a relational database is modeled following ideal practices (e.g., 3NF), then the resulting knowledge graph from a direct mapping may be an adequate start. However, enterprise relational databases are complex and inscrutable, thus the resulting knowledge graph from a directly mapped enterprise relational database is also going to be inscrutable.

Direct Mapping to RDF Graphs

The W3C has standardized a direct mapping from relational databases to RDF Graphs [M. Arenas, 2012]. The W3C Direct Mapping consists of two parts: a specification for generating identifiers for the different components of the database schema, and a specification for using the identifiers, in order to generate a direct graph.

Generating Identifiers: The W3C Direct Mapping generates an identifier for rows, tables, columns, and foreign keys. If a table has a primary key, then the row identifier will be an IRI, obtained by concatenating a base IRI, the percent-encoded form of the table name, the "#" character and for each column in the primary key, in order:

- the percent-encoded form of the column name,

- the "=" character,

- the percent-encoded representation of the column value, and

- if it is not the last column in the primary key, the ";" character.

If a table does not have a primary key, then the row identifier is a fresh blank node that is unique to each row.

The IRI for a table is obtained by concatenating the base IRI with the percent-encoded form of the table name. The IRI for an attribute is obtained by concatenating the base IRI with the percent-encoded form of the table name, the "#" character and the percent-encoded form of the column name. Finally, the IRI for foreign key is obtained by concatenating the base IRI with the percent-encoded form of the table name, the string "#ref-" and for each column in the foreign key, in order:

- the percent-encoded form of the column name and

- if it is not the last column in the foreign key, a ";" character.

Generating the Direct Graph: A Direct Graph is the RDF graph resulting from directly mapping each of the rows of each table and each view in a database schema. Each row in a table generates a Row Graph. The row graph is an RDF graph consisting of the following triples: (1) a row type triple, (2) a literal triple for each column in a table where the column value is non-NULL, and (3) a reference triple for each foreign key in the table where none of the column values is NULL. A row type triple is an RDF triple with the subject as the row node for the row, the predicate as the RDF IRI `rdf:type` and the object as the table IRI for the table name. A literal triple is an RDF triple with the subject as the row node for the row, the predicate as the literal property IRI for the column, and the object as the natural RDF literal representation of the column value. Finally, a reference triple is an RDF triple with the subject as the row node for the row, the predicate as the reference property IRI for the columns and the object as the row node for the referenced row.

2.3.2   CUSTOM MAPPING

A Custom Mapping is a customizable representation of a relational database as a knowledge graph. The body of the mapping rule is a SQL query on the relational database and the head of the rule represents elements of the knowledge graph schema: Concepts, Concept Attributes, Relationships, and Relationship Attributes. The knowledge graph schema can be created or reused (as discussed in Section 2.2.3).

Concept Mappings
A concept mapping is a representation of a concepts in the knowledge graph from the relational database. It is represented as follows:

$$\text{SELECT ID FROM ...}$$
$$\Longrightarrow$$
$$(\text{template-}\{\underline{\text{ID}}\}) - \text{type} \rightarrow (\text{Concept})$$

Every row resulting from the SQL query and uniquely identified by the attribute ID represents an instance of the concept.

Example 2.5
Source: The table `customer_entity` stores data about all customers. The column `is_active` indicates if a customer is active or not.

customer_entity		
entity_id	email	is_active
100	juan@	1
101	ora@	1
102	alice@	0

Target: In the Knowledge Graph, the schema consists of the concept (Customer).

$$(\text{Customer})$$

The meaning of a customer is if they are active, therefore the expected Knowledge Graph is the following:

$$(\text{customer-1}) - \text{type} \rightarrow (\text{Customer})$$
$$(\text{customer-2}) - \text{type} \rightarrow (\text{Customer})$$

Mapping: To generate the knowledge graph, the definition of *Customer* is represented in a SQL query that filters on `is_active = 1`

SELECT entity_id FROM customer_entity WHERE is_active = 1
$$\Longrightarrow$$
$(\text{customer-}\{\underline{\texttt{entity\_id}}\}) - \text{type} \rightarrow (\text{Customer})$

Concept Attribute Mappings

A concept attribute mapping is a representation of an attribute associated to a concept in the knowledge graph from the relational database. It is represented as follows:

SELECT ID, ATTR FROM ...
$$\Longrightarrow$$
$(\text{template-}\{\underline{\texttt{ID}}\}) - \text{conceptAttribute} \rightarrow [\{\texttt{ATTR}\}]$

Every row resulting from the SQL query and uniquely identified by the attribute ID, has a corresponding attribute which represents a concept attribute in the knowledge graph.

Example 2.6

Source: The `sales_flat_order` table stores all the order transactions.

sales_flat_order			
entity_id	grand_total	tax_amount	discount_amount
1	110	8.8	1.2
2	100	10	0

Target: The knowledge graph schema consists of the concept *Order* and an associated attribute *netsales* whose datatype is a float.

$$(\text{Order}) - \text{netsales} \rightarrow [\text{float}]$$

The business defines *netsales* by taking the grand total and subtracting the tax and discount. Therefore, the expected knowledge graph is the following:

$$(\text{order-1}) - \text{netsales} \rightarrow [100]$$
$$(\text{order-2}) - \text{netsales} \rightarrow [90]$$

Mapping: To generate the knowledge graph, the definition of *netsales* is represented in the SQL query. The mapping is the following:

```
SELECT entity_id, grand_total - tax_amount - discount_amount as net
FROM sales_flat_order
```
$$\Longrightarrow$$
$$(\text{order-}\{\underline{\texttt{entity\_id}}\}) -\text{netsales} \rightarrow [\{\text{net}\}]$$

Relationship Mappings

A concept attribute mapping is a representation of an attribute associated to a concept in the knowledge graph from the relational database.

A relationship mapping is a representation of a relationship between two concepts in the knowledge graph from the relational database. It is represented as follows:

```
SELECT ID1,ID2 FROM ...
```
$$\Longrightarrow$$
$$(\text{template1-}\{\underline{\texttt{ID1}}\}) -\text{relationship} \rightarrow (\text{template2-}\{\underline{\texttt{ID2}}\})$$

Every row resulting from the SQL query represents a relationship between two concepts that are uniquely identified by ID1 and ID2, respectively.

Example 2.7
Source: The `sales_flat_order` table stores all the order transactions. The column `entity_id` is the primary key. The column `customer_id` is a foreign key that references the `customer_entity` table and associates the customers to the orders.

sales_flat_order	
entity_id	customer_id
1	100
2	100

Target: The knowledge graph schema consists of the concepts *Order* and *Customer*. The relationship *placed by* connects the *Order* concept to *Customer* concept.

$$(\text{Order}) -\text{placedBy} \rightarrow (\text{Customer})$$

The expected knowledge graph is the following:

$$(\text{order-1}) -\text{placedBy} \rightarrow (\text{customer-100})$$
$$(\text{order-2}) -\text{placedBy} \rightarrow (\text{customer-100})$$

Mapping: The relationship mapping is from the foreign key column `customer_id` from the table `sales_flat_order` to the relationship *placedBy*. The mapping is the following:

> SELECT entity_id,customer_id FROM sales_flat_order
> $$\Longrightarrow$$
> (order-{entity_id}) $-$placedBy$\rightarrow$ (customer-{customer_id})

Relationship Attribute Mappings

A relationship attribute mapping is a representation of an attribute associated with a relationship between two concepts in the knowledge graph from the relational database. It is represented as follows:

> SELECT ID1, ID2, ATTR FROM ...
> $$\Longrightarrow$$
> (template1-{ID1}) $-$relationship[relAttr $=$ "{ATTR}"]$\rightarrow$ (template2-{ID2})

Every row resulting from the SQL query represents a relationship between two concepts that are uniquely identified by ID1 and ID2, respectively, and has a corresponding attribute ATTR which represents the relationship attribute in the knowledge graph.

Example 2.8

Source: The customer_rel table is a many-to-many table that represents a relationship when two customers connect with each other. The table has columns customer_id1 and customer_id2 which are foreign keys that references the customer_entity table, and a column created_at which represents when the two customers connected.

customer_rel			
entity_id	customer_id1	customer_id2	created_at
10	100	101	2009-01-01

Target: The knowledge graph schema consists of the concepts *Customer* and the relationship *knows* connects a *Customer* concept with itself. The relationship attribute *since* is associated to the *knows* relationship

> (Customer) $-$knows{since $=$ [date]}$\rightarrow$ (Customer)

The expected knowledge graph is the following:

> (customer-100) $-$knows{since $=$ [2009-01-01]}$\rightarrow$ (customer-101)

Mapping: To generate the knowledge graph, the *knows* relationship is represented in the SQL query that projects the customer_id1 and customer_id2 which are the identifiers for customers. The relationship attribute mapping is from the column created_at to the relationship attribute *since* associated with the relationship *knows*. The mapping is the following:

```
SELECT customer_id1, customer_id2, created_at FROM customer_rel
```
$$\Longrightarrow$$
$$(\text{customer-}\{\underline{\texttt{customer\_id1}}\}) -\text{knows}\{\text{since} = [\{\text{created\_at}\}]\}$$
$$\rightarrow \big[\text{customer-}\{\underline{\texttt{customer\_id2}}\}\big]$$

2.3.3   MAPPING LANGUAGES

We have presented the mappings in an abstract notation. In practice, these mappings need to be implemented in a language that can then be executed. The mappings can be implemented in a programming language (e.g., Java, Python). We present two declarative languages to implement the mappings. Given the declarative nature of SQL, it can also be used to implement the mappings to a knowledge graph. For RDF Knowledge Graphs, there exists a W3C recommendation: R2RML, the *Relational Database to RDF Mapping Language.*

SQL as a Mapping Language
Mappings are rules. Queries are rules. Views are named queries. SQL is a query language. Therefore, mappings can be represented in SQL.[6] Recall that a mapping rule is represented as follows:

$$
\begin{array}{c}
\texttt{<condition>} \\
\Longrightarrow \\
\texttt{<conclusion>}
\end{array}
$$

The mapping rule would represented in SQL as follows:

```
SELECT  <conclusion>
FROM (  <condition> )
```

Executing these SQL queries will return the corresponding elements of the knowledge graph, in other words, it would be a materialization approach. This is a viable way to test mappings before implementing in a mapping language such as R2RML (see next subsection), etc.

Example 2.9
Concept Mapping in SQL from Example 2.5

```
SELECT
    concat('customer-',entity_id) as s,
    'type' p,
```

---

[6]We acknowledge the irony. However, representing mappings in SQL is used for quick-and-dirty implementations.

```
    'Customer' o
FROM (
  SELECT entity_id FROM customer_entity WHERE is_active = 1
)
```

Example 2.10
Concept Attribute Mapping in SQL from Example 2.6

```
SELECT
    concat('order-',entity_id) as s,
    'netsales' p,
    net o
FROM (
 SELECT entity_id, grand_total - tax_amount - discount_amount as net
 FROM sales_flat_order
)
```

Example 2.11
Relationship Mapping in SQL from Example 2.7

```
SELECT
    concat('order-',entity_id) s,
    'placedBy' p,
    concat('customer-',customer_id) o
FROM (
 SELECT entity_id, customer_id FROM sales_flat_order
)
```

Example 2.12
Relationship Attribute Mapping in SQL from Example 2.8

```
SELECT
    concat('customer-',customer_id1) s,
    concat('knows{since=',created_at, '}') p,
    concat('customer-',customer_id2) o
```

```
FROM (
  SELECT customer_id1, customer_id2, created_at FROM customer_rel
)
```

Relational Database to RDF Mapping Language (R2RML)

R2RML[7] [Das, 2012] is a language for expressing customized mappings from relational databases to RDF graphs expressed in a graph structure and schema of the user's choice. R2RML is a W3C recommendation. An R2RML mapping is itself represented as an RDF graph. Turtle is the recommended syntax for writing R2RML mappings.

RML[8] is an unofficial extension to R2RML that supports mappings to CSV, JSON, and XML. Recall that the focus of this book is on relational databases as a source, however, the principles presented in this book also apply to mappings in RML.

The R2RML language features can be divided in two parts: features for generating RDF terms (IRIs, blank nodes, or literals) and features for generating RDF triples.

Generating RDF Terms: An RDF term is either an IRI, a blank node, or a literal. A term map generates an RDF term for the subjects, predicates, and objects of the RDF triples from either a constant, a template or a column value. A constant-valued term map ignores the row and always generates the same RDF term. A column-valued term map generates an RDF term from the value of a column. A template-valued term map generates an RDF term from a string template, which is a format string that can be used to build strings from multiple components, including the values of a column. Template-valued term maps are commonly used to specify how an IRI should be generated.

The R2RML language allows a user to explicitly state the type of RDF term that needs to be generated (IRI, blank node or literal). If the RDF term is for a subject, then the term type must be either an IRI or blank Node. If the RDF term is for a predicate, then the term type must be an IRI. If the RDF term is for a object, then the term type can be either an IRI, blank node or literal. Additionally, a developer may assert that a literal has an assigned language tag or datatype.

Generating RDF Triples: RDF triples are derived from a logical table. A logical table can be either a base table or view in the relational schema, or an R2RML view. An R2RML view is a logical table whose contents are the result of executing a SQL SELECT query against the input database.

---

[7]https://www.w3.org/TR/r2rml/
[8]https://rml.io/specs/rml/

A triples map is the heart of an R2RML mapping. It specifies a rule for translating each row of a logical table to RDF triples. A triples map is represented by a resource that references the following other resources

- It must have exactly one logical table. Its value is a logical table that specifies a SQL query result to be mapped to triples.

- It must have exactly one subject map that specifies how to generate a subject for each row of the logical table.

- It may have zero or more predicate-object maps, which specify pairs of predicate maps and object maps that, together with the subject generated by the subject map, may form one or more RDF triples for each row.

Recall that there are three types of term maps that generate RDF terms: constant-valued, column-valued, and template-valued. Given that a subject, predicate and object of an RDF triple must be RDF terms, this means that a subject, predicate, and object can be any of the three possible term maps, called subject map, predicate map, and object map, respectively. A predicateObject map groups predicate-object map pairs.

A subject map is a term map that specifies the subject of the RDF triple. The primary key of a table is usually the basis for creating an IRI. Therefore, it is normally the case that a subject map is a template-valued term map with an IRI template using the value of a column which is usually the primary key. Optionally, a subject map may have one or more class IRIs. For each RDF term generated by the subject map, RDF triples with predicate `rdf:type` and the class IRI as object will be generated.

A predicate-object map is a function that creates one or more predicate-object pairs for each row of a logical table. It is used in conjunction with a subject map to generate RDF triples in a triples map. A predicate-object map is represented by a resource that references the following other resources: one or more predicate maps and one or more object maps or referencing object maps.

A predicate map is a term map. It is common that the predicate of an RDF triple is a constant. Therefore, a predicate map is usually a constant-valued term map. An object map is also a term map. Several use cases may arise where the object could be either a constant-valued, template-valued or column-valued term map.

For further details, we refer the reader to Das [2012].

Example 2.13

Concept Mapping in R2RML from Example 2.5, expressed using Turtle syntax:

```
:AConceptMapping a rr:TriplesMap ;
rr:subjectMap [
```

```
    rr:template "customer-{entity_id}"
    rr:class :Customer ;
] ;
rr:logicalTable [
   rr:sqlQuery "SELECT entity_id FROM customer_entity
          WHERE is_active = 1"
] .
```

Example 2.14

Concept Attribute Mapping in R2RML from Example 2.6

```
:AConceptAttributeMapping a rr:TriplesMap ;
rr:subjectMap [
  rr:template "order-{entity_id}"
] ;
rr:predicateObjectMap[
   rr:predicate :netsales;
   rr:objectMap [ rr:column "netsales" ] ;
];
rr:logicalTable [
   rr:sqlQuery """
      SELECT entity_id, grand_total - tax_amount -
          discount_amount as netsales
      FROM sales_flat_order
   """
] .
```

Example 2.15

Relationship Mapping in R2RML from Example 2.7

```
:ARelationshipMapping a rr:TriplesMap ;
rr:subjectMap [
  rr:template "order-{entity_id}";
] ;
rr:predicateObjectMap[
   rr:predicate :placedBy;
```

```
    rr:objectMap [ rr:template "customer-{customer_id}" ] ;
  ];
  rr:logicalTable [
    rr:tableName "sales_flat_order"
  ].
```

CHAPTER 3

Mapping Design Patterns

In software engineering, a design pattern is a general repeatable solution within a given context. A design pattern describes a template on how to solve a problem that can be reused in various situations. Design patterns are best practices to help solve common problems and speed up development processes.

Inspired by software design patterns, we present mapping design patterns, reusable mapping templates that solve a commonly occurring problem. Reusing mapping design patterns can help prevent subtle issues that may cause problems down the line and improve readability of the mappings by other developers. It is important to note that this is not an exhaustive list of mapping design patterns.

These mapping patterns provide a playbook to (1) map relational databases to Concepts, Attributes, and Relationships of the knowledge graph and (2) define the identifiers of the entities in the knowledge graph.

The first type of custom mappings are **direct custom mappings**. A custom mapping is direct if there is a 1:1 correspondence between the following:

Relational Database	Knowledge Graph
Table	Concept
Column	(Concept/Relationship) Attribute
Foreign Key	Relationship

The direct custom mappings are direct mappings with the ability to custom define the target, instead of creating the knowledge graph schema based on the source relational schema.

A second type of custom mappings are **complex custom mappings**. A custom mapping is complex if an arbitrary SQL query is required.

The rest of the chapter presents a series of mapping design patterns.

3.1 DIRECT CUSTOM MAPPING PATTERNS

3.1.1 DIRECT CONCEPT

Context: A table in the relational database represents a concept in the knowledge graph. This means that every single row of the table, which is uniquely identified by the primary key column(s) represents an instance of a concept. Therefore, the direct concept mapping is from the table to a concept.

Solution: The table and the corresponding primary key are mapped to a concept

$$
\text{SELECT } \underline{\text{ID}} \text{ FROM TABLE}
$$
$$
\Longrightarrow
$$
$$
(\text{template-}\{\underline{\text{ID}}\}) -\text{type}\rightarrow (\text{Concept})
$$

where $\underline{\text{ID}}$ is the primary key column of the table `TABLE`.

Example 3.1

Source: The `sales_flat_order` table stores all the order transactions.

sales_flat_order	
entity_id	grand_total
1	110
2	100

Target: In the knowledge graph, the schema consists of the concept *Order*.

$$(Order)$$

The expected knowledge graph is the following:

$$
(\text{order-1}) -\text{type}\rightarrow (\text{Order})
$$
$$
(\text{order-2}) -\text{type}\rightarrow (\text{Order})
$$

Mapping:

$$
\text{SELECT } \underline{\text{entity\_id}} \text{ FROM sales\_flat\_order}
$$
$$
\Longrightarrow
$$
$$
(\text{order-}\{\underline{\text{entity\_id}}\}) -\text{type}\rightarrow (\text{Order})
$$

This example is visually represented in Figure 3.1.

3.1.2 DIRECT CONCEPT ATTRIBUTE

Context: A table in the relational database represents a concept in the knowledge graph and a column of that table represents an attribute associated with the concept in the knowledge graph. This means that every single row of the table, which is uniquely identified by the primary key column(s) of that table, represents an instance of representative Concept and the given column of that table represents the attribute associated with the Concept. Therefore, the direct concept attribute mapping is from a column in a table to a concept attribute (and there is also a direct concept mapping from the table to the concept).

Solution: The table and the corresponding primary key is mapped to a concept

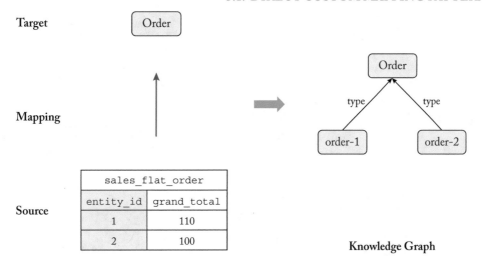

Figure 3.1: Direct concept mapping example.

$$\text{SELECT } \underline{\text{ID}}, \text{ COL FROM TABLE}$$
$$\Longrightarrow$$
$$(\text{template-}\{\underline{\text{ID}}\}) - \text{conceptAttribute} \rightarrow [\{\text{COL}\}]$$

where $\underline{\text{ID}}$ is the primary key column of the table TABLE.

Example 3.2

Source: The sales_flat_order table stores all the order transactions.

sales_flat_order	
entity_id	order_currency_code
1	USD
2	EUR

Target: The knowledge graph schema consists of the concept *Order* and an associated attribute *Currency* whose datatype is a string:

$$(\text{Order}) - \text{currency} \rightarrow [\text{string}]$$

The expected knowledge graph is the following:

$$(\text{order-1}) - \text{currency} \rightarrow [\text{USD}]$$
$$(\text{order-2}) - \text{currency} \rightarrow [\text{EUR}]$$

Mapping: The direct concept attribute mapping is from the column order_currency_code from the table sales_flat_order to the concept attribute *Currency*. The mapping is the following:

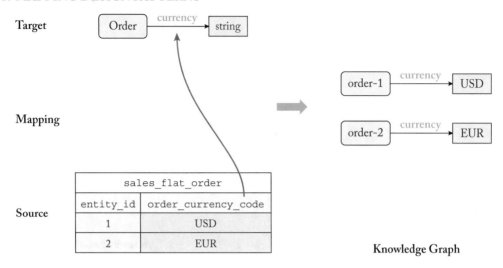

Figure 3.2: Direct concept attribute mapping example.

```
SELECT entity_id, order_currency_code FROM sales_flat_order
                          ⟹
    (order-{entity_id}) −currency→ [order_currency_code]
```

This example is visually represented in Figure 3.2.

3.1.3 DIRECT RELATIONSHIP

Context: A foreign key attribute of a table represents a relationship in the knowledge graph. This means that every pair of primary key and foreign key attributes per row in the table represents an instance of the relationship between a Concept that is identified by the primary key and another Concept that is identified by the foreign key. Therefore, the direct relationship mapping is from a foreign key to a relationship.

Solution: The table with corresponding primary key and the column which is a foreign key is mapped to a relationship

```
            SELECT PK, FK FROM TABLE
                       ⟹
    (template1-{PK}) −relationship→ (template2-{FK})
```

where PK is the primary key column of the table TABLE and FK is a foreign key column that references another table.

Example 3.3

Source: The `sales_flat_order` table stores all the order transactions. The column `entity_id` is the primary key. The column `customer_id` is a foreign key that references the `customer_entity` table and associates the customers to the orders.

sales_flat_order	
entity_id	customer_id
1	100
2	100

Target: The knowledge graph schema consists of the concepts *Order* and *Customer*. The relationship *placed by* connects the *Order* concept to *Customer* concept.

$$(Order) - placedBy \rightarrow (Customer)$$

The expected knowledge graph is the following:

$$(order\text{-}1) - placedBy \rightarrow (customer\text{-}100)$$
$$(order\text{-}2) - placedBy \rightarrow (customer\text{-}100)$$

Mapping: The direct relationship mapping is from the foreign key column `customer_id` from the table `sales_flat_order` to the relationship *placedBy*. The mapping is the following:

SELECT entity_id, customer_id FROM sales_flat_order
$$\Longrightarrow$$
(order-{entity_id}) − placedBy → (customer-{customer_id})

This example is visually represented in Figure 3.3.

3.1.4 DIRECT RELATIONSHIP ATTRIBUTE

Context: A foreign key attribute of a table represents a relationship in the knowledge graph. This means that every pair of primary key and foreign key attributes per row in the table represents an instance of the relationship between a Concept that is identified by the primary key and another Concept that is identified by the foreign key. Additionally, there is an additional column in the table that represents a relationship attribute. Therefore, the direct relationship attribute mapping is from a column that qualifies a foreign key to a relationship attribute.

Solution: The table with corresponding primary key and the column which is a foreign key is mapped to a relationship

SELECT PK, FK, COL FROM TABLE
$$\Longrightarrow$$
(template1-{PK}) − relationship{relattr = [COL]} → (template2-{FK})

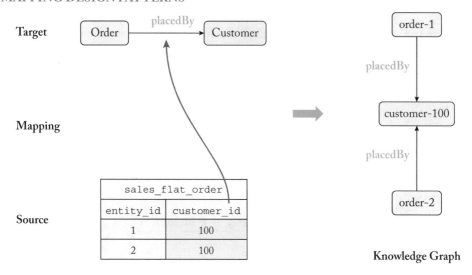

Figure 3.3: Direct relationship mapping example.

where <u>PK</u> is the primary key column of the table TABLE and <u>FK</u> is a foreign key column that references another table.

Example 3.4
Source: The sales_flat_order table stores all the order transactions. The column entity_id is the primary key. The column customer_id is a foreign key that references the customer_entity table and associates the customers to the orders. The column created_at represents the time that the customer started to create the order.

sales_flat_order		
entity_id	customer_id	created_at
1	100	2021-01-01T09:00:00
2	100	2021-01-02T09:30:00

Target: The knowledge graph schema consists of the concepts *Order* and *Customer*. The relationship *placedBy* connects the *Order* concept to *Customer* concept. The attribute *startTime* is associated to the *placedBy* relationship

$$(\text{Order}) -\text{placedBy}\{\text{startTime} = [\text{datetime}]\} \rightarrow (\text{Customer})$$

The expected knowledge graph is the following:

$$(\text{order-1}) -\text{placedBy}\{\text{startTime} = [2021\text{-}01\text{-}01\text{T}09\text{:}00\text{:}00]\} \rightarrow (\text{customer-100})$$
$$(\text{order-2}) -\text{placedBy}\{\text{startTime} = [2021\text{-}01\text{-}02\text{T}09\text{:}30\text{:}00]\} \rightarrow (\text{customer-100})$$

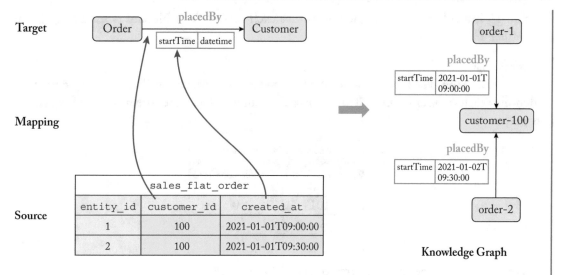

Figure 3.4: Direct relationship attribute example.

Mapping: The direct relationship attribute mapping is from the column `created_at` from the table `sales_flat_order` to the relationship attribute *startTime* associated with the relationship *placedBy*. The mapping is the following:

$$\text{SELECT } \underline{\texttt{entity\_id}}, \ \underline{\texttt{customer\_id}}, \ \underline{\texttt{created\_at}} \text{ FROM } \texttt{sales\_flat\_order}$$
$$\Longrightarrow$$
$$(\text{order-}\{\underline{\texttt{entity\_id}}\}) - \text{placedBy}\{\text{startTime} = [\{\text{created\_at}\}]\} \rightarrow (\text{customer-}\{\underline{\texttt{customer\_id}}\})$$

This example is visually represented in Figure 3.4.

3.2 COMPLEX CUSTOM CONCEPT MAPPING PATTERNS

3.2.1 COMPLEX CONCEPT: CONDITIONS

Context: A subset of the rows in a table represents a concept in the knowledge graph.

Solution: Define a query needs to be defined that returns the specific rows through a condition that satisfies the definition of the concept

$$\text{SELECT } \underline{\text{ID}} \text{ FROM TABLE WHERE CONDITION}$$
$$\Longrightarrow$$
$$(\text{template-}\{\underline{\text{ID}}\}) - \text{type} \rightarrow (\text{Concept})$$

where ID is a column that uniquely identifies each row of the table and is used to create an identifier TABLE.

Example 3.5

Source: The sales_flat_order table stores all the order transactions. The entity_id uniquely identifies each order. However, if the transaction enters a bad state, the entity_id values are negative.

sales_flat_order	
entity_id	grand_total
-100	0
-101	0
1	110
2	100

Target: The knowledge graph schema consists of the concept *Order*.

$$\boxed{(Order)}$$

The expected knowledge graph is the following:

$$\boxed{\begin{array}{l} (\text{order-1}) - \text{type} \rightarrow (\text{Order}) \\ (\text{order-2}) - \text{type} \rightarrow (\text{Order}) \end{array}}$$

Mapping:

$$\boxed{\begin{array}{c} \texttt{SELECT entity\_id FROM sales\_flat\_order WHERE entity\_id > 0} \\ \Longrightarrow \\ (\text{order-}\{\texttt{entity\_id}\}) - \text{type} \rightarrow (\text{Order}) \end{array}}$$

This example is visually represented in Figure 3.5.

3.2.2   COMPLEX CONCEPT: DATA AS A CONCEPT

Context: A subset of the rows in a table, defined by an enumeration of values over a specific column, represents a concept in the knowledge graph.

Solution: Define a query that returns the specific rows through a condition on specific values of a column that satisfies the definition of the concept

$$\boxed{\begin{array}{c} \texttt{SELECT ID FROM TABLE WHERE COL IN (A, B, C, ...)} \\ \Longrightarrow \\ (\text{template-}\{\underline{\texttt{ID}}\}) - \text{type} \rightarrow (\text{Concept}) \end{array}}$$

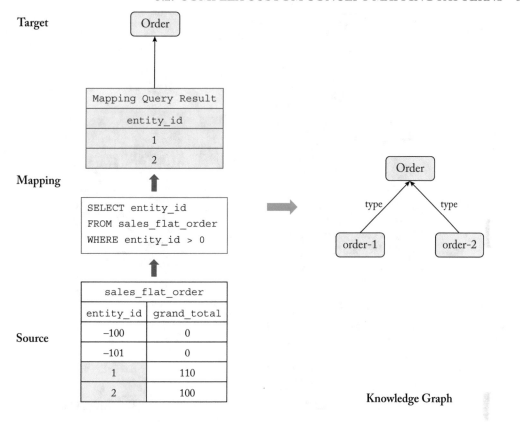

Figure 3.5: Complex custom concept mapping: condition example.

where ID is a column that uniquely identifies each row of the table and is used to create an identifier TABLE.

Example 3.6

Source: The sales_flat_order table stores all the order transactions. The column status contains the status of the order, such as pending, complete, processing, etc.

sales_flat_order	
entity_id	status
1	pending
2	complete
3	processing

Target: The knowledge graph schema consists of the concept *PendingOrder*.

(*PendingOrder*)

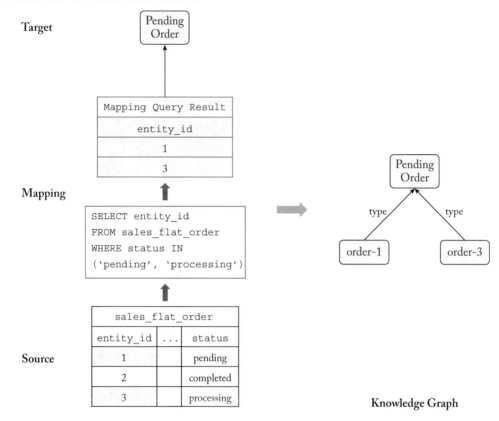

Figure 3.6: Complex custom concept mapping: data as a class example.

The expected knowledge graph is the following:

$$(\text{order-1}) -\text{type} \rightarrow (\text{PendingOrder})$$
$$(\text{order-3}) -\text{type} \rightarrow (\text{PendingOrder})$$

Mapping:

```
SELECT entity_id FROM sales_flat_order
WHERE status IN ('pending', 'processing')
```
$$\Longrightarrow$$
$$(\text{order-}\{\underline{\texttt{entity\_id}}\}) -\text{type} \rightarrow (\text{PendingOrder})$$

This example is visually represented in Figure 3.6.

Discussion: Similar to the Conditions design pattern. In this case, the condition is specific to enumeration of values associated to a column.

3.2.3   COMPLEX CONCEPT: JOIN

Context: A concept in the knowledge graph spans multiple tables in the relational databases.

Solution: Define a query the joins the multiple tables

```
SELECT ID
FROM TABLE1
JOIN TABLE2 ON ...
```
$$\Longrightarrow$$
$$(\text{template-}\{\underline{ID}\}) -\text{type}\rightarrow (\text{Concept})$$

where $\underline{ID}$ is a column that uniquely identifies each row of the resulting query result and is used to create the identifier.

Example 3.7

Source: The `sales_flat_order` table stores all the order transactions and `sales_flat_order_payment` stores all the orders that have payments processed. The column `entity_id` of the `sales_flat_order_payment` table is a foreign key that references `sales_flat_order`.

sales_flat_order	
entity_id	...
1	
2	
3	
4	

sales_flat_order_payment	
entity_id	...
1	
2	
3	

Target: The knowledge graph schema consists of the concept *Order*.

$$(\textit{Order})$$

The business defines an Order as order transactions that have a payment processed. Therefore, the expected knowledge graph is the following:

$$(\text{order-1}) -\text{type}\rightarrow (\text{Order})$$
$$(\text{order-2}) -\text{type}\rightarrow (\text{Order})$$
$$(\text{order-3}) -\text{type}\rightarrow (\text{Order})$$

Mapping: The tables `sales_flat_order` and `sales_flat_order_payment` need to be joined and the result are mapped to the *Order* concept in the knowledge graph. The mapping is the following:

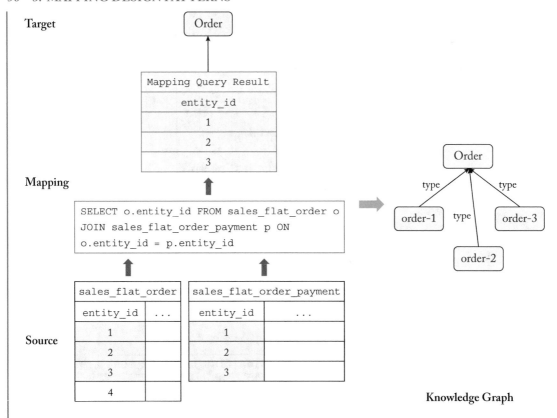

Figure 3.7: Complex custom concept mapping: join example.

```
SELECT o.entity_id
FROM sales_flat_order o
JOIN sales_flat_order_payment p
ON o.entity_id = p.entity_id
              ⟹
(order-{entity_id}) −type→ (Order)
```

This example is visually represented in Figure 3.7.

Discussion: A LEFT/RIGHT/OUTER JOIN are not considered because they would not constrain the original table. If that is the case, then no joins would be needed.

3.2.4   COMPLEX CONCEPT: DISTINCT

Context: A table represents more than one concept in the knowledge graph. For one of the concepts, the rows that represent the concepts appear duplicated in the table.

Solution: Define a query that returns the distinct rows that represents the concept, ideally with an attribute that serves as a key that uniquely identifies each distinct row that represents a concept

> SELECT DISTINCT <u>ID</u> FROM TABLE
> $$\Longrightarrow$$
> $(\text{template-}\{\underline{ID}\}) - \text{type} \rightarrow (\text{Concept})$

where <u>ID</u> is a column that uniquely identifies each row of the resulting query and is used to create an identifier for the concept.

Example 3.8

Source: The `sales_flat_order` table stores all the order transactions. The column `status` contains the status of the order, such as pending, complete, processing, etc.

sales_flat_order			
entity_id	...	customer_id	first_name
1		100	Juan
2		100	Juan
3		101	Ora

Target: The knowledge graph schema consists of the concept *Customer*.

> (*Customer*)

The expected knowledge graph is the following:

> $(\text{customer-100}) - \text{type} \rightarrow (\text{Customer})$
> $(\text{customer-101}) - \text{type} \rightarrow (\text{Customer})$

Mapping:

> SELECT DISTINCT customer_id FROM sales_flat_order
> $$\Longrightarrow$$
> $(\text{customer-}\{\underline{\texttt{customer\_id}}\}) - \text{type} \rightarrow (\text{Customer})$

This example is visually represented in Figure 3.8.

Discussion: This appears when a table is a denormalized view (i.e., multiple tables have been joined and values get repeated).

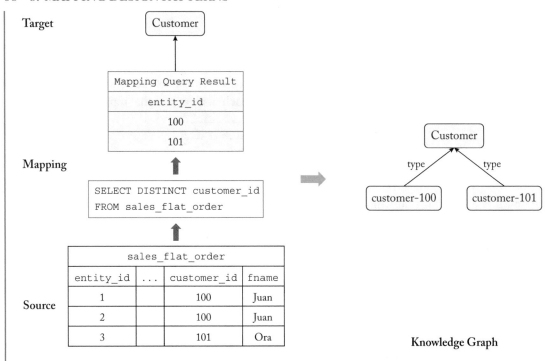

Figure 3.8: Complex custom concept mapping: distinct example.

3.3   COMPLEX CUSTOM ATTRIBUTE MAPPING PATTERNS

The following attribute mapping patterns can be applied to either Concepts or Relationships.

3.3.1   COMPLEX CONCEPT ATTRIBUTE: CONCAT

Context: Multiple columns need to be concatenated in order to represent the attribute.

Solution: Use the SQL CONCAT function

$$\text{SELECT } \underline{ID}, \text{ CONCAT(COL1, COL2, ...) AS } \underline{COL} \text{ FROM TABLE}$$
$$\Longrightarrow$$
$$(\text{template-}\{\underline{ID}\}) - \text{conceptAttribute} \rightarrow [\{\underline{COL}\}]$$

where $\underline{ID}$ is a column that uniquely identifies each row of the resulting query and is used as the identifier for the attribute's associated concept.

Example 3.9

Source: The `customer_entity` table stores all the customers. The customer names are stored by first name and last name.

customer_entity		
entity_id	first_name	last_name
100	Juan	Sequeda
101	Ora	Lassila

Target: The knowledge graph schema consists of the concept *Customer* and an associated attribute *name* which represents a full name, and whose datatype is a string.

$$\boxed{(\text{Order}) - \text{currency} \rightarrow [\text{string}]}$$

The expected knowledge graph is the following:

$$\text{(customer-100)} - \text{name} \rightarrow [\text{Juan Sequeda}]$$
$$\text{(customer-101)} - \text{name} \rightarrow [\text{Ora Lassila}]$$

Mapping: The columns `first_name` and `last_name` need to be concatenated with a space in between. The mapping is the following:

```
SELECT entity_id, concat(first_name, ' ', last_name) as fullname
FROM customer_entity
```
$$\Longrightarrow$$
$$\text{(customer-}\{\underline{\text{entity\_id}}\}) - \text{name} \rightarrow [\{\underline{\text{fullname}}\}]$$

This example is visually represented in Figure 3.9.

3.3.2 COMPLEX CONCEPT ATTRIBUTE: MATH

Context: Values in different columns need to be applied in a math formula in order to be mapped to an attribute.

Solution: Use the SQL arithmetic operators and math functions

```
SELECT ID, COL1+COL2 AS COL FROM TABLE
```
$$\Longrightarrow$$
$$\text{(template-}\{\underline{\text{ID}}\}) - \text{conceptAttribute} \rightarrow [\{\underline{\text{COL}}\}]$$

where `ID` is a column that uniquely identifies each row of the resulting query and is used as the identifier for the attribute's associated concept.

Example 3.10

Source: The `sales_flat_order` table stores all the order transactions.

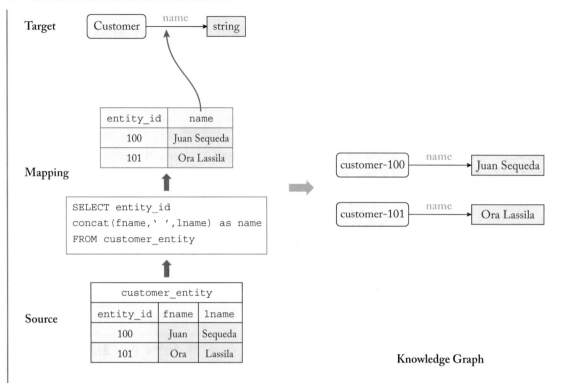

Figure 3.9: Complex custom attribute mapping: CONCAT example.

sales_flat_order			
entity_id	grand_total	tax_amount	discount_amount
1	110	8.8	1.2
2	100	10	0

Target: The knowledge graph schema consists of the concept *Order* and an associated attribute *netsales* whose datatype is a float.

$$(\text{Order}) - \text{netsales} \rightarrow [\text{float}]$$

The business defines *netsales* by taking the grand total and subtracting the tax and discount. Therefore, the expected knowledge graph is the following:

$$(\text{order-1}) - \text{netsales} \rightarrow [100]$$
$$(\text{order-2}) - \text{netsales} \rightarrow [90]$$

Mapping: To generate the knowledge graph, the definition of *netsales* is represented in the SQL query. The mapping is the following:

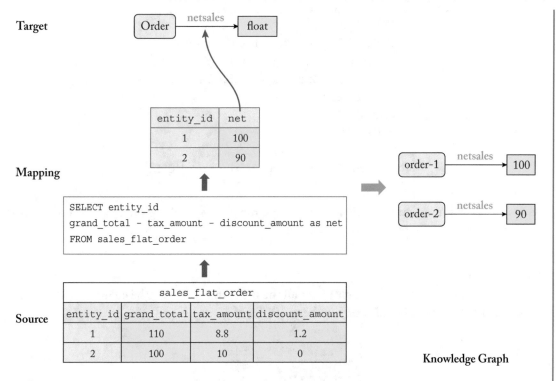

Figure 3.10: Complex custom attribute mapping: math example.

```
SELECT entity_id, grand_total - tax_amount - discount_amount as net
FROM sales_flat_order
                            ⟹
              (order-{entity_id}) −netsales→ [{net}]
```

This example is visually represented in Figure 3.10.

3.3.3   COMPLEX CONCEPT ATTRIBUTE: CASE

Context: Values in a column are codes and each code needs to be mapped to a certain constant.

Solution: Use the SQL CASE statement to represent the mapping to each fixed value. The entire case statement is mapped to the attribute

```
SELECT ID,
CASE WHEN condition1 THEN result1
     WHEN condition2 THEN result2
     WHEN conditionN THEN resultN
     ELSE result
END AS COL
FROM TABLE
```

$$\Longrightarrow$$

$$(\text{template-}\{\underline{ID}\}) - \text{conceptAttribute} \rightarrow [\{\underline{COL}\}]$$

where $\underline{ID}$ is a column that uniquely identifies each row of the resulting query and is used as the identifier for the attribute's associated concept.

Example 3.11

Source: The `sales_flat_order` table stores all the order transactions. The column `status` contains the status of the order as code numbers: 10, 11, etc.

sales_flat_order		
entity_id	...	status
1		10
2		11
3		10

Target: The knowledge graph schema consists of the concept *Order* and an associated attribute *orderStatus* whose datatype is a string:

$$(\text{Order}) - \text{orderStatus} \rightarrow [\text{string}]$$

The order status 10 means Closed and 11 means Pending. The expected knowledge graph is the following:

$$(\text{order-1}) - \text{orderStatus} \rightarrow [\text{Pending}]$$
$$(\text{order-2}) - \text{orderStatus} \rightarrow [\text{Closed}]$$
$$(\text{order-3}) - \text{orderStatus} \rightarrow [\text{Pending}]$$

Mapping: To generate the knowledge graph, the correspondence of 10 to Closed and 11 to processing is represented in a SQL CASE statement. The mapping is the following:

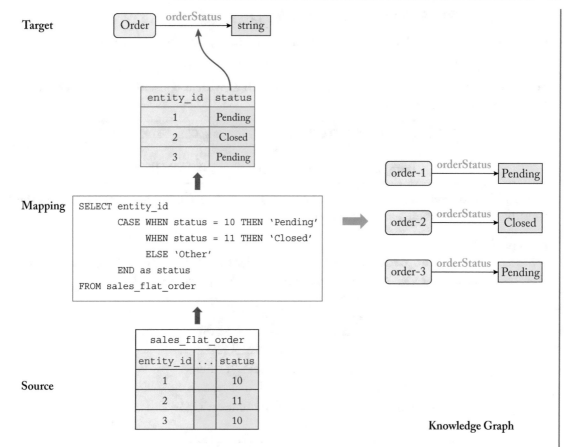

Figure 3.11: Complex custom attribute mapping: CASE example.

```
SELECT entity_id,
CASE WHEN status = 10 THEN 'Pending'
     WHEN status = 11 THEN 'Closed'
     ELSE 'Other'
END AS status
FROM sales_flat_order
            ⟹
(order-{entity_id}) −orderStatus→ [{status}]
```

This example is visually represented in Figure 3.11.

3.3.4 COMPLEX CONCEPT ATTRIBUTE: NULL

Context: A column can have a NULL, which should be replaced by a constant in order to be mapped to an attribute.

Solution: Use a SQL function that replaces a NULL with a constant such as `IFNULL()`, `ISNULL()`, `COALESCE()`, or `NVL()`

> SELECT <u>ID</u>, COALESCE(COL1, 'VALUE') as COL FROM TABLE
> $$\Longrightarrow$$
> (template-{<u>ID</u>}) $-$conceptAttribute$\rightarrow$ [{<u>COL</u>}]

where <u>ID</u> is a column that uniquely identifies each row of the resulting query and is used as the identifier for the attribute's associated concept.

Example 3.12

Source: The `sales_flat_order` table stores all the order transactions. The column `status` contains the status of the order, such as Closed, Processing, etc., including `NULL`.

sales_flat_order		
entity_id	...	status
1		Pending
2		Closed
3		NULL

Target: The knowledge graph schema consists of the concept *Order* and an associated attribute *orderStatus* whose datatype is a string:

> (Order) $-$orderStatus$\rightarrow$ [string]

A `NULL` status means unknown. The expected knowledge graph is the following:

> (order-1) $-$orderStatus$\rightarrow$ [Pending]
> (order-2) $-$orderStatus$\rightarrow$ [Closed]
> (order-3) $-$orderStatus$\rightarrow$ [Unknown]

Mapping: To generate the knowledge graph, the correspondence of NULL to Unknown is represented in a SQL COALESCE function. The mapping is the following:

> SELECT entity_id, COALESCE(status, 'Unknown') as status
> FROM sales_flat_order
> $$\Longrightarrow$$
> (order-{<u>entity_id</u>}) $-$orderStatus$\rightarrow$ [{<u>status</u>}]

This example is visually represented in Figure 3.12.

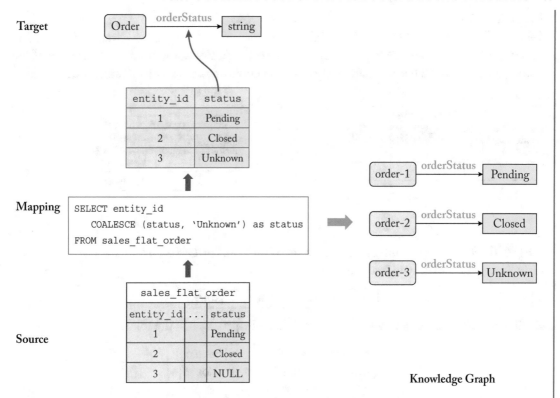

Figure 3.12: Complex custom attribute mapping: NULL example.

3.3.5   COMPLEX CONCEPT ATTRIBUTE: JOIN

Context: The identifier of the concept is in one table while the column that needs to be mapped is in a different table.

Solution: Join the tables together such that the identifier of the concept and the column to be mapped is in the same relation

$$
\begin{aligned}
&\texttt{SELECT } \underline{\texttt{t1.ID}}, \texttt{t2.COL} \\
&\texttt{FROM TABLE1 t1} \\
&\texttt{JOIN TABLE2 t2 on t1.a = t2.a} \\
&\Longrightarrow \\
&(\text{template-}\{\underline{\text{ID}}\}) - \text{conceptAttribute} \rightarrow [\{\underline{\text{COL}}\}]
\end{aligned}
$$

where $\underline{\text{ID}}$ is a column that uniquely identifies each row of the resulting query and is used as the identifier for the attribute's associated concept.

Example 3.13

Source: The `sales_flat_order` table stores all the order transactions. The `sales_order_status` stores the look up codes of order statuses. The column `status_id` of the `sales_flat_order` table is a foreign key that references `entity_id` of `sales_order_status`.

sales_flat_order		
entity_id	...	status_id
1		10
2		11
3		10

sales_order_status	
entity_id	status
10	Pending
11	Closed

Target: The knowledge graph schema consists of the concept *Order* and an associated attribute *orderStatus* whose datatype is a string:

$$\text{(Order)} -\text{orderStatus} \rightarrow \text{[string]}$$

A `NULL` status means unknown. The expected knowledge graph is the following:

$$\text{(order-1)} -\text{orderStatus} \rightarrow \text{[Pending]}$$
$$\text{(order-2)} -\text{orderStatus} \rightarrow \text{[Closed]}$$
$$\text{(order-3)} -\text{orderStatus} \rightarrow \text{[Pending]}$$

Mapping: The tables `sales_flat_order` and `sales_order_status` need to be joined in order to associate the status column of `sales_order_status` with the orders in `sales_flat_order`. The mapping is the following:

```
SELECT entity_id, status
FROM sales_flat_order o
JOIN sales_order_status s ON o.status_id = s.entity_id
```
$$\Longrightarrow$$
$$\text{(order-\{entity\_id\})} -\text{orderStatus} \rightarrow \text{[\{status\}]}$$

This example is visually represented in Figure 3.13.

3.3.6   COMPLEX CONCEPT ATTRIBUTE: LEFT JOIN

Context: The identifier of the concept is in one table while the column that needs to be mapped is in a different table. However, the join keys may have NULL values.

Solution: Join the tables together using LEFT JOIN such that the identifier of the concept and the column to be mapped is in the same relation. Then apply the NULL mapping pattern

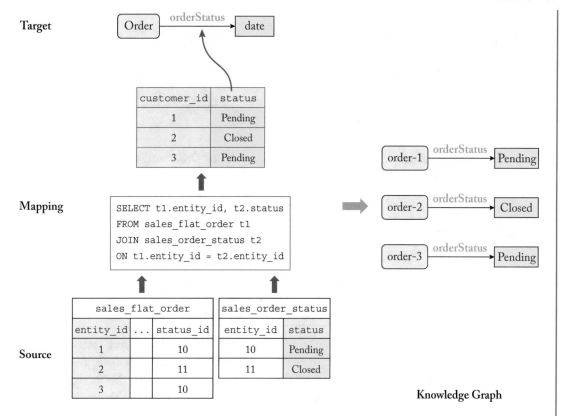

Figure 3.13: Complex custom attribute mapping: JOIN example.

```
SELECT t1.ID, COALESCE(t2.COL, 'VALUE') AS COL
              FROM TABLE1 t1
     LEFT JOIN TABLE2 t2 ON t1.a = t2.a
                  ⟹
   (template-{ID}) −conceptAttribute→ [{COL}]
```

where ID is a column that uniquely identifies each row of the resulting query and is used as the identifier for the attribute's associated concept.

Example 3.14

Source: The sales_flat_order table stores all the order transactions. The sales_order_status stores the look up codes of order statuses. The column status_id of the sales_flat_order table is a foreign key that references entity_id of sales_order_status.

sales_flat_order		
entity_id	...	status_id
1		10
2		11
3		11
4		NULL

sales_order_status	
entity_id	status
10	Processing
11	Closed

Target: The knowledge graph schema consists of the concept *Order* and an associated attribute *orderStatus* whose datatype is a string:

$$(Order) -orderStatus \rightarrow [string]$$

A NULL status means unknown. The expected knowledge graph is the following:

$$(order\text{-}1) -orderStatus \rightarrow [Pending]$$
$$(order\text{-}2) -orderStatus \rightarrow [Closed]$$
$$(order\text{-}3) -orderStatus \rightarrow [Closed]$$
$$(order\text{-}4) -orderStatus \rightarrow [Unknown]$$

Mapping: The tables sales_flat_order and sales_order_status need to be joined in order to associate the status column of sales_order_status with the orders in sales_flat_order. It has to be a left join in order to not reject the rows with NULL value in the foreign key column. Additionally, the resulting NULL should be replaced with "Unknown." The mapping is the following:

```
SELECT entity_id, COALESCE(status, 'Unknown') status
FROM sales_flat_order o
LEFT JOIN sales_order_status s ON o.status_id = s.entity_id
```
$$\Longrightarrow$$
$$(order\text{-}\{\underline{entity\_id}\}) -orderStatus \rightarrow [\{\underline{status}\}]$$

This example is visually represented in Figure 3.14.

Discussion: Why does this happen? All orders should have an order status, right? The NULL value is probably indicative of a data quality issue.

3.3.7   COMPLEX CONCEPT ATTRIBUTE: DUPLICATE

Context: A table (or the result of a query) already contains the identifier of the concept and the column that is to be mapped to an attribute. However, there the identifier of the concept is not serving as a key because multiple rows exist with the same identifier but with different values of the colum.

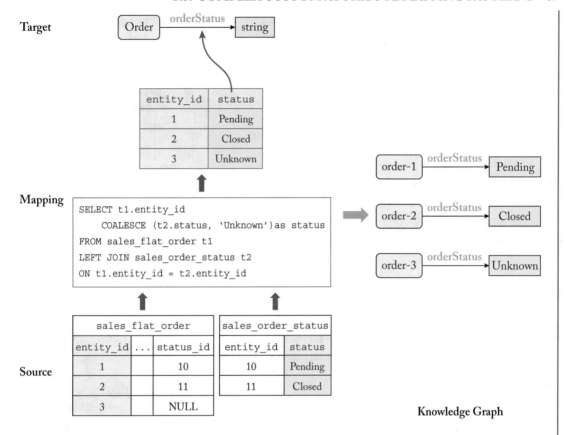

Figure 3.14: Complex custom attribute mapping: LEFT JOIN example.

Solution: Use an aggregator function (MIN or MAX) and group by the identifier of the concept, in order to guarantee uniqueness

$$
\begin{array}{c}
\texttt{SELECT \underline{ID}, MIN(COL1) AS \underline{COL}} \\
\texttt{FROM TABLE} \\
\texttt{GROUP BY ID} \\
\Longrightarrow \\
(\text{template-}\{\underline{ID}\}) - \text{conceptAttribute} \rightarrow [\{\underline{COL}\}]
\end{array}
$$

where $\underline{ID}$ is a column that uniquely identifies each row of the resulting query and is used as the identifier for the attribute's associated concept.

Example 3.15

Source: The `customer_date` table stores all data about customers and dates: when they joined, their birthdate, etc. The column `entity_id` is the primary key, `customer_id` is a foreign key that references the `customer_entity` table. Even though the database does not violate any integrity constraints, there is a data quality issue because `customer_id` has two birthdates: 1985-10-17 and 1986-10-17.

customer_date				
entity_id	customer_id	date_value	join_date	birth_date
1	1	2020-01-01	1	0
2	1	1985-10-17	0	1
3	1	1986-10-17	0	1
4	2	2020-01-01	1	0
5	2	1980-01-01	0	1

Target: The knowledge graph schema consists of the concept *Customer* and an associated attribute *birthDate* whose datatype is a date:

$$(\text{Customer}) - \text{birthDate} \rightarrow [\text{date}]$$

The expected knowledge graph is the following:

$$(\text{customer-1}) - \text{birthDate} \rightarrow [1985 - 10 - 17]$$
$$(\text{customer-2}) - \text{birthDate} \rightarrow [1980 - 01 - 01]$$

Mapping: To generate the knowledge graph, we need to eliminate the duplicate birthdate. However, it is not known which is the correct birth date. We can do an aggregation over the date_value and arbitrarily choose between MIN or a MAX. The mapping is the following:

```
SELECT customer_id, MIN(date_value) as birthdate
FROM sales_flat_order
WHERE birthdate = 1
GROUP BY customer_id
```
$$\Longrightarrow$$
$$(\text{customer-}\{\underline{\text{entity\_id}}\}) - \text{birthDate} \rightarrow [\{\underline{\text{birthdate}}\}]$$

This example is visually represented in Figure 3.15.

Discussion: Why does this happen? We are masking the data quality problem in the mappings.

3.3.8   COMPLEX CONCEPT ATTRIBUTE: CONSTANT TABLE

Context: A table name represents the value that needs to be mapped to an attribute.

Solution: Project the concept identifier from the table and the constant that the table is representing which is to be mapped to the attribute

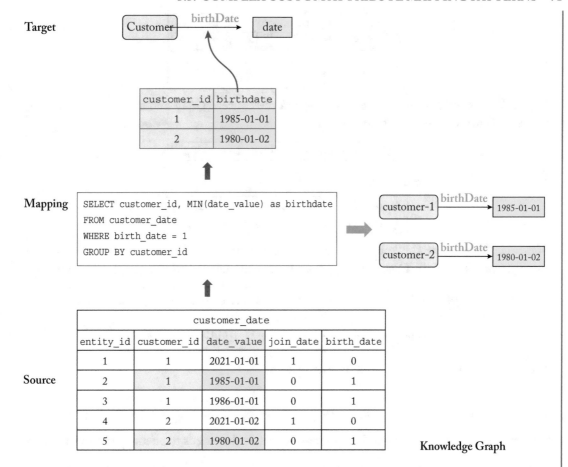

Figure 3.15: Complex custom attribute mapping: duplicate example.

$$\text{SELECT } \underline{\text{ID}}, \text{ 'CONSTANT' AS } \underline{\text{COL}} \text{ FROM TABLE}$$
$$\Longrightarrow$$
$$(\text{template-}\{\underline{\text{ID}}\}) - \text{conceptAttribute} \rightarrow [\{\underline{\text{COL}}\}]$$

where <u>ID</u> is a column that uniquely identifies each row of the resulting query and is used as the identifier for the attribute's associated concept.

Example 3.16

Source: The `sales_flat_order_payment_paypal` table stores all the payment transactions that came through the Paypal payment platform:

sales_flat_order_payment_paypal	
entity_id	amount_paid
1	110
2	100

Target: The knowledge graph schema consists of the concept *Order* and an associated attribute *paymentMethod* whose datatype is a string:

$$(Order) - paymentMethod \rightarrow [string]$$

The expected knowledge graph is the following:

$$(order\text{-}1) - paymentMethod \rightarrow [Paypal]$$
$$(order\text{-}2) - paymentMethod \rightarrow [Paypal]$$

Mapping: To generate the knowledge graph, a constant value "Paypal" is added to each row coming from the sales_flat_order_payment_paypal table. The mapping is the following:

SELECT entity_id, 'Paypal' AS method FROM sales_flat_payment_paypal
$$\Longrightarrow$$
(order-{entity_id}) − paymentMethod → [{method}]

This example is visually represented in Figure 3.16.

3.3.9 COMPLEX CONCEPT ATTRIBUTE: CONSTANT ATTRIBUTE

Context: A column name in a table represents the value that needs to be mapped to an attribute.

Solution: Project the concept identifier from the table and filter by the column that represents the attribute. Provide a constant that the column is representing which is to be mapped to the attribute

SELECT ID, 'CONSTANT' AS COL
FROM TABLE
WHERE CONSTANT = VALUE
$$\Longrightarrow$$
(template-{ID}) − conceptAttribute → [{COL}]

where ID is a column that uniquely identifies each row of the resulting query and is used as the identifier for the attribute's associated concept.

Example 3.17

Source: The sales_flat_order_payment table stores all the payment transactions and has a flag to know from which payment system it came from:

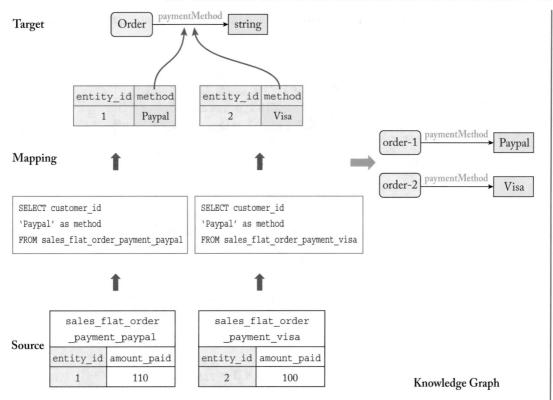

Figure 3.16: Complex custom attribute mapping: constant table.

sales_flat_order_payment				
entity_id	amount_paid	paypal	visa	mc
1	110	1	0	0
2	100	0	1	0

Target: The knowledge graph schema consists of the concept *Order* and an associated attribute *paymentMethod* whose datatype is a string:

$$(Order) -paymentMethod \rightarrow [string]$$

The expected knowledge graph is the following:

$$(order\text{-}1) -paymentMethod \rightarrow [Paypal]$$
$$(order\text{-}2) -paymentMethod \rightarrow [Paypal]$$

Mapping: To generate the knowledge graph, a constant value "Paypal" is added to each row coming from the sales_flat_order_payment table where paypal=1, and a constant value

"Visa" is added to each row coming from the `sales_flat_order_payment` table where `visa=1`. The mappings are the following:

Mapping for Paypal

$$\begin{array}{c} \texttt{SELECT entity\_id, 'Paypal' AS \underline{method}} \\ \texttt{FROM sales\_flat\_payment} \\ \texttt{WHERE paypal = 1} \\ \Longrightarrow \\ (\text{order-}\{\underline{\texttt{entity\_id}}\}) -\text{paymentMethod} \rightarrow [\{\underline{\texttt{method}}\}] \end{array}$$

Mapping for Visa

$$\begin{array}{c} \texttt{SELECT entity\_id, 'Visa' AS \underline{method}} \\ \texttt{FROM sales\_flat\_payment} \\ \texttt{WHERE visa = 1} \\ \Longrightarrow \\ (\text{order-}\{\underline{\texttt{entity\_id}}\}) -\text{paymentMethod} \rightarrow [\{\underline{\texttt{method}}\}] \end{array}$$

This example is visually represented in Figure 3.17.

Discussion: We could also add paypal = 1 and visa = 0 to assure data quality.

3.3.10 COMPLEX CONCEPT ATTRIBUTE: CONSTANT VALUE

Context: A value in a column is a code and it needs to be mapped to a certain constant.

Solution: Project the concept identifier from the table and filter by value in the column that represents the attribute. Provide a constant that the value is representing which is to be mapped to the attribute

$$\begin{array}{c} \texttt{SELECT \underline{ID}, 'CONSTANT' AS \underline{COL}} \\ \texttt{FROM TABLE} \\ \texttt{WHERE type = 'CONSTANT'} \\ \Longrightarrow \\ (\text{template-}\{\underline{\texttt{ID}}\}) -\text{conceptAttribute} \rightarrow [\{\underline{\texttt{COL}}\}] \end{array}$$

where ID is a column that uniquely identifies each row of the resulting query and is used as the identifier for the attribute's associated concept.

Example 3.18

Source: The `sales_flat_order_payment` table stores all the payment transactions and has a flag to know from which payment system it came from:

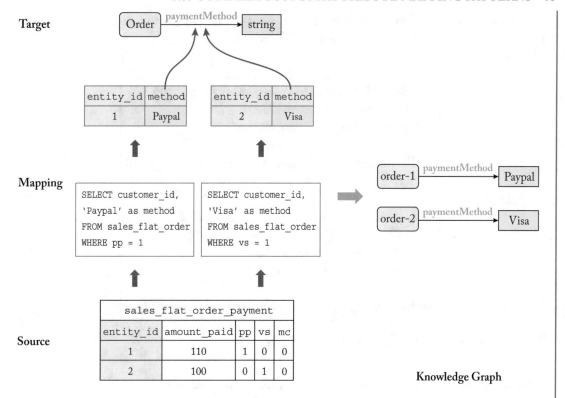

Figure 3.17: Complex custom attribute mapping: constant attribute.

sales_flat_order_payment		
entity_id	amount_paid	payment_type
1	110	pp
2	100	vs

Target: The knowledge graph schema consists of the concept *Order* and an associated attribute *paymentMethod* whose datatype is a string:

$$(Order) - paymentMethod \rightarrow [string]$$

The expected knowledge graph is the following:

$$(order\text{-}1) - paymentMethod \rightarrow [Paypal]$$
$$(order\text{-}2) - paymentMethod \rightarrow [Paypal]$$

Mapping: To generate the knowledge graph, a constant value "Paypal" is added to each row coming from the sales_flat_order_payment table where payment_type = pp, and a constant value "Visa" is added to each row coming from the sales_flat_order_payment table where payment_type = vs. The mappings are the following:

Mapping for Paypal

```
SELECT entity_id, 'Paypal' AS method
FROM sales_flat_payment
WHERE payment_type = 'pp'
```
$$\Longrightarrow$$
$$(\text{order-}\{\underline{\texttt{entity\_id}}\}) - \text{paymentMethod} \rightarrow [\{\underline{\texttt{method}}\}]$$

Mapping for Visa

```
SELECT entity_id, 'Visa' AS method
FROM sales_flat_payment
WHERE payment_type = 'vs'
```
$$\Longrightarrow$$
$$(\text{order-}\{\underline{\texttt{entity\_id}}\}) - \text{paymentMethod} \rightarrow [\{\underline{\texttt{method}}\}]$$

This example is visually represented in Figure 3.18.

Discussion: This is a specific version of the CASE mapping pattern.

3.3.11   COMPLEX CONCEPT ATTRIBUTE: EAV

Context: The relational data is represented in a entity–attribute–value (EAV) model where the attributes of an entity and the corresponding value are all data values in a table.

Solution: The attribute is mapped to value in the attribute column and the entity and value columns are projected

```
SELECT ENTITY_ID, VALUE FROM EAV_TABLE
      WHERE ATTRIBUTE = 'CONSTANT'
```
$$\Longrightarrow$$
$$(\text{template-}\{\underline{\texttt{ENTITY\_ID}}\}) - \text{conceptAttribute} \rightarrow [\{\underline{\texttt{VALUE}}\}]$$

where ENTITY_ID is a column that uniquely identifies each row of the resulting query and is used as the identifier for the attribute's associated concept.

Example 3.19
Source: The customer_eav_varchar table stores attribute and values that are varchars for customer-related data

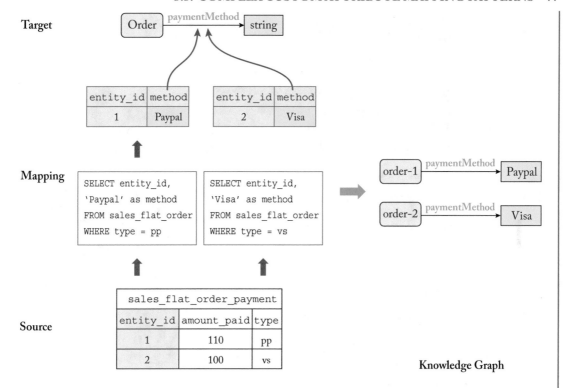

Figure 3.18: Complex custom attribute mapping: constant attribute.

customer_eav_varchar		
entity_id	attribute_id	value
100	1	Juan
100	2	Sequeda
100	3	juan@data.world
101	1	Ora
101	2	Lassila
101	3	ora@amazon.com

Target: The knowledge graph schema consists of the concept *Customer* and an associated attribute *email* and whose datatype is a string.

$$(Order) -email\rightarrow [string]$$

The expected knowledge graph is the following:

$$(customer\text{-}100) -email\rightarrow [juan@data.world]$$
$$(customer\text{-}101) -email\rightarrow [ora@amazon.com]$$

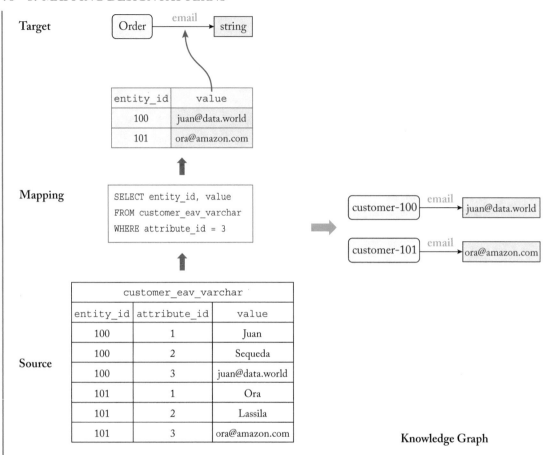

Figure 3.19: Complex custom attribute mapping: EAV.

Mapping: The mapping is the following:

SELECT entity_id, value FROM customer_eav_varchar WHERE attribute_id = 3
$$\Longrightarrow$$
(customer-{entity_id}) −email→ [{value}]

This example is visually represented in Figure 3.19.

Discussion: An EAV model is used to enable flexibility given that the relational model is rigid. A triple table, which is a way of storing graph data in a relational database, is a form of an EAV model.

3.4   COMPLEX CUSTOM RELATIONSHIP MAPPING PATTERNS

3.4.1   RELATIONSHIP: MANY TO MANY

Context: A table represents a many-to-many relationship when it is modeled by having two foreign keys that reference the corresponding entities that are being related. The table can have additional attributes. This means that the pair of foreign keys attributes per row in the table represents an instance of the relationship between Concepts that are identified by the foreign key.

Solution: An ordered pair of foreign keys from the many-to-many table are mapped to a relationship

$$
\text{SELECT FK1, FK2 FROM TABLE}
$$
$$
\Longrightarrow
$$
$$
(\text{template1-}\{\underline{FK1}\}) -\text{relationship} \rightarrow (\text{template2-}\{\underline{FK2}\})
$$

where $\underline{FK1}$ and $\underline{FK2}$ are foreign key columns that references other tables.

Example 3.20

Source: The `customer_shipping_address` table stores the many to many relationship of customers and shipping address. The column `customer_id` is a foreign key that references a customer table and the column `shipping_address_id` is a foreign key that references an address table. Both columns form a primary key.

customer_shipping_address	
customer_id	shipping_address_id
100	1000
100	1001
101	1002
101	1000

Target: The knowledge graph schema consists of the concepts *Customer* and *Address*. The relationship *has shipping address* connects the *Customer* concept to *Address* concept.

$$
(\text{Customer}) -\text{hasShippingAddress} \rightarrow (\text{Address})
$$

The expected knowledge graph is the following:

$$
(\text{customer-100}) -\text{hasShippingAddress} \rightarrow (\text{address-1000})
$$
$$
(\text{customer-100}) -\text{hasShippingAddress} \rightarrow (\text{address-1001})
$$
$$
(\text{customer-101}) -\text{hasShippingAddress} \rightarrow (\text{address-1002})
$$
$$
(\text{customer-101}) -\text{hasShippingAddress} \rightarrow (\text{address-1000})
$$

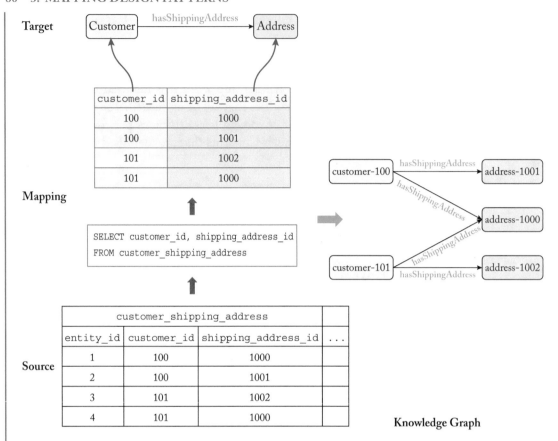

Figure 3.20: Relationship: many to many.

Mapping:

> SELECT <u>customer_id</u>, <u>shipping_address_id</u> FROM customer_shipping_address
> $$\Longrightarrow$$
> (customer-{<u>customer_id</u>}) −hasShippingAddress→ (address-{<u>shipping_address_id</u>})

This example is visually represented in Figure 3.20.

Discussion: The direction of the relationship was established going from Order to an Address. An inverse relationship can use the same body of the mapping rule. The head of the mapping rule would have the order of the foreign key columns swapped.

3.4.2   RELATIONSHIP: ONE TO MANY WITHOUT DUPLICATES

Context: A table contains data that represents two concepts and the relationship between them. There is no redundancy in the table which means that the primary key of the table can serve as part of the unique identifier for each concept.

Solution: Create three mappings, one for the first concept, another one for the second concept and a final one for the relationship. All three mappings use the same key

$$\begin{array}{c} \text{SELECT } \underline{\text{ID}} \text{ FROM TABLE} \\ \Longrightarrow \\ (\text{template1-}\{\underline{\text{ID}}\}) -\text{type} \rightarrow (\text{Concept1}) \end{array}$$

$$\begin{array}{c} \text{SELECT } \underline{\text{ID}} \text{ FROM TABLE} \\ \Longrightarrow \\ (\text{template2-}\{\underline{\text{ID}}\}) -\text{type} \rightarrow (\text{Concept2}) \end{array}$$

$$\begin{array}{c} \text{SELECT } \underline{\text{ID}} \text{ FROM TABLE} \\ \Longrightarrow \\ (\text{template1-}\{\underline{\text{ID}}\}) -\text{relationship} \rightarrow (\text{template2-}\{\underline{\text{ID}}\}) \end{array}$$

where $\underline{\text{ID}}$ is a column that uniquely identifies each row of the resulting query and is used as the identifier for Concept1 and Concept2.

Example 3.21

Source: The `customer_entity` table stores all the customers and their addresses. The column `entity_id` is the primary key.

customer_entity					
entity_id	fname	lname	street	city	state
1	Juan	Sequeda	123 A St.	Austin	TX
2	Ora	Lassila	456 B St.	Austin	TX

Target: The knowledge graph schema consists of the concepts *Customer* and *Address*. The relationship *hasAddress* connects the *Customer* concept to *Address* concept.

$$(\text{Customer}) -\text{hasAddress} \rightarrow (\text{Address})$$

The expected knowledge graph is the following:

$$\begin{array}{c} (\text{customer-1}) -\text{type} \rightarrow (\text{Customer}) \\ (\text{customer-2}) -\text{type} \rightarrow (\text{Customer}) \\ (\text{address-1}) -\text{type} \rightarrow (\text{Address}) \\ (\text{address-2}) -\text{type} \rightarrow (\text{Address}) \\ (\text{customer-1}) -\text{hasAddress} \rightarrow (\text{address-1}) \\ (\text{customer-2}) -\text{hasAddress} \rightarrow (\text{address-2}) \end{array}$$

Mapping: To generate the knowledge graph, we use the entity_id primary key column to uniquely identify the Customer and Address. We have to make sure that the identifier is globally unique and this is done by prefixing a string "customer" and "address" under the assumption that those strings will be part of the identifiers for Customer and Address, respectively. The mapping is the following:

$$\frac{\texttt{SELECT entity\_id FROM customer\_entity}}{(\text{customer-}\{\texttt{entity\_id}\}) - \text{type} \rightarrow (\text{Customer})}$$

$$\frac{\texttt{SELECT entity\_id FROM customer\_entity}}{(\text{address-}\{\texttt{entity\_id}\}) - \text{type} \rightarrow (\text{Address})}$$

$$\frac{\texttt{SELECT entity\_id FROM customer\_entity}}{(\text{customer-}\{\texttt{entity\_id}\}) - \text{hasAddress} \rightarrow (\text{address-}\{\texttt{entity\_id}\})}$$

This example is visually represented in Figure 3.21.

Discussion: This is the process of denormalizing a table into two tables and establishing a foreign key between them.

3.4.3 RELATIONSHIP: ONE TO MANY WITH DUPLICATES

Context: A table contains data that represents two concepts and the relationship between them. However, there is redundancy in the table which means that the primary key of the table can serve as part of the unique identifier for one concept. There may be another value that can serve as identifier for the second concept but that appears repeated.

Solution: Create three mappings, one for the first concept using the key of the table, another one for the second concept by definition distinct to get the unique key, and a final one for the relationship

$$\frac{\texttt{SELECT ID1 FROM TABLE}}{(\text{template1-}\{\texttt{ID1}\}) - \text{type} \rightarrow (\text{Concept1})}$$

$$\frac{\texttt{SELECT DISTINCT ID2 FROM TABLE}}{(\text{template2-}\{\texttt{ID2}\}) - \text{type} \rightarrow (\text{Concept2})}$$

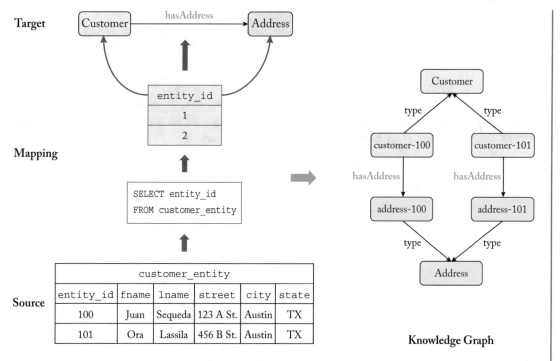

Figure 3.21: Relationship: one to many without duplicates example.

$$\text{SELECT } \underline{ID1}, \underline{ID2} \text{ FROM TABLE}$$
$$\Longrightarrow$$
$$(\text{template1-}\{\underline{ID1}\}) -\text{relationship}\rightarrow (\text{template2-}\{\underline{ID2}\})$$

where $\underline{ID1}$ is a column that uniquely identifies each row of the resulting query and is used as the identifier for Concept1. $\underline{ID2}$ is a column that uniquely identifies the rows that will mapped to Concept2.

Example 3.22

Source: The `sales_flat_order` table stores all the order transactions and the customer data. The customer data is redundant because it is repeated for each order transaction. The column `entity_id` is the primary key for the `sales_flat_order` table. The column `customer_id` uniquely identifies a customer, however it is repeated (as with all the other customer data) in the `sales_flat_order` table.

sales_flat_order				
entity_id	grand_total	customer_id	fname	lname
1	110	100	Juan	Sequeda
2	100	100	Juan	Sequeda
3	95	101	Ora	Lassila

Target: The knowledge graph schema consists of the concepts *Order* and *Customer*. The relationship *placedBy* connects the *Order* concept to *Customer* concept.

$$(\text{Order}) -\text{placedBy} \rightarrow (\text{Customer})$$

The expected knowledge graph is the following:

$$(\text{customer-100}) -\text{type} \rightarrow (\text{Customer})$$
$$(\text{customer-101}) -\text{type} \rightarrow (\text{Customer})$$
$$(\text{order-1}) -\text{type} \rightarrow (\text{Order})$$
$$(\text{order-2}) -\text{type} \rightarrow (\text{Order})$$
$$(\text{order-3}) -\text{type} \rightarrow (\text{Order})$$
$$(\text{order-1}) -\text{placedBy} \rightarrow (\text{customer-100})$$
$$(\text{order-2}) -\text{placedBy} \rightarrow (\text{customer-100})$$
$$(\text{order-3}) -\text{placedBy} \rightarrow (\text{customer-101})$$

Mapping: To generate the knowledge graph, the Order concept is direct custom mapping to the sales_flat_order table, while the Customer concept is mapped to the distinct customer_id of the sales_flat_order table. Finally, the placedBy relationship is mapped to the column pair (entity_id, customer_id). The mapping is the following:

```
SELECT entity_id FROM sales_flat_entity
```
$$\Longrightarrow$$
$$(\text{order-\{\underline{entity\_id}\}}) -\text{type} \rightarrow (\text{Order})$$

```
SELECT DISTINCT customer_id FROM sales_flat_entity
```
$$\Longrightarrow$$
$$(\text{customer-\{\underline{customer\_id}\}}) -\text{type} \rightarrow (\text{Customer})$$

```
SELECT entity_id, customer_id FROM sales_flat_entity
```
$$\Longrightarrow$$
$$(\text{order-\{\underline{entity\_id}\}}) -\text{placedBy} \rightarrow (\text{customer-\{\underline{entity\_id}\}})$$

This example is visually represented in Figure 3.22.

Discussion: This is the process of denormalizing a table into two tables and establishing a foreign key between them.

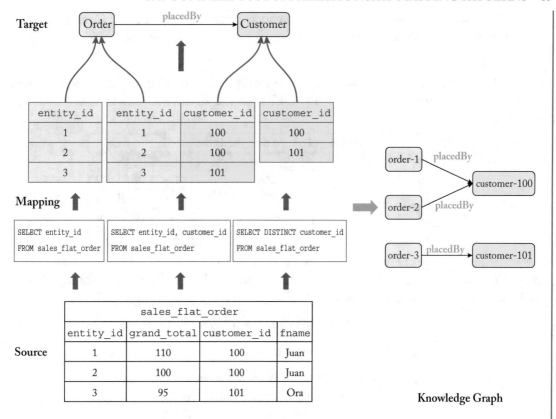

Figure 3.22: Relationship: one to many without duplicates example.

3.4.4   RELATIONSHIP: ONE TO ONE WITH DUPLICATES

Context: A table contains data that represents a 1-1 relationship between two concepts. However, the table stores data with a 1-M cardinality.

Solution: Create a subquery that returns a 1-1 relationship from the table by grouping on the attribute that has duplicate data. Decide which function (MIN, MAX) needs to be applied and on which column based on the usecase. The subquery is then joined with the table

```
SELECT A.ID1, A.ID2
FROM TABLE A
JOIN (SELECT ID1, MAX(COL) AS MAXCOL FROM TABLE GROUP BY ID1) B
ON A.ID1 = B.ID1 AND A.COL = B.MAXCOL
                    ⟹
        (template1-{ID1}) −relationship→ (template2-{ID2})
```

where $\underline{\text{ID1}}$ is a column that is used to create the identifier for the instances of Concept1. $\underline{\text{ID2}}$ is a column that is used to create the identifier for the instances of Concept2.

Example 3.23

Source: The `sales_flat_order_address` table stores all the shipping address data associated to an order transaction. If the shipping address has been updated, then a new tuple is added to the table.

sales_flat_order_address			
entity_id	order_id	address_id	created_at
10	1	1000	2021-01-01 08:00:00
11	1	1002	2021-01-01 08:30:00
12	2	1001	2021-01-01 09:00:00
13	3	1000	2021-01-01 10:00:00

Target: The knowledge graph schema consists of the concepts *Order* and *Address*. The relationship *shippedTo* connects the *Order* concept to *Address* concept. Additionally, the business logic is that an order can only be shipped to one address, hence it is a 1-1 relationship:

$$(\text{Order}) -\text{shippedTo} \rightarrow (\text{Address})$$

The expected knowledge graph is the following:

$$(\text{order-1}) -\text{shippedTo} \rightarrow (\text{address-1002})$$
$$(\text{order-2}) -\text{shippedTo} \rightarrow (\text{address-1001})$$
$$(\text{order-3}) -\text{shippedTo} \rightarrow (\text{address-1000})$$

Mapping: To generate the knowledge graph, the shippedTo relationship needs to be mapped to the column pair (order_id,address_id). However, note that there may be duplicates. In this example, order_id=1 has two different address_id, 1000 and 1002, and this violates the business logic. In order to return a 1-1 relationship, the SQL query must aggregate all the order_id and address_id by some qualifier, in this case, the maximum created_at. The mapping is the following:

```
SELECT A.order_id, A.address_id
FROM sales_flat_order_address A
JOIN (SELECT order_id, MAX(created_at) AS MAXCOL
FROM sales_flat_order_address GROUP BY order_id) B
ON A.order_id = B.order_id AND A.created_at = B.MAXCOL
                    ⟹
  (order-{order_id}) -shippedTo → (address-{address_id})
```

This example is visually represented in Figure 3.23.

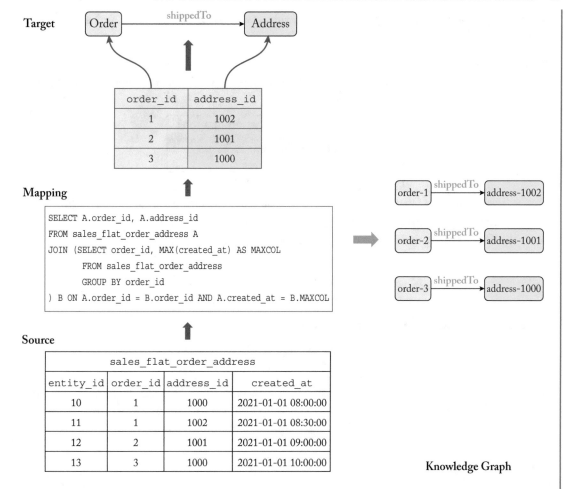

Figure 3.23: Relationship: one to one with duplicates.

3.4.5   RELATIONSHIP: CONSTANT TABLE

Context: A table name represents the value that needs to be mapped to a relationship and a corresponding concept.

Solution: Create a query that returns the identifier used to create instances of the domain of the relationship and define a constant that maps to the range concept of the relationship

$$\text{SELECT } \underline{ID}, \text{ 'constant' AS } \underline{CONCEPT} \text{ FROM TABLE}$$
$$\Longrightarrow$$
$$(\text{template-}\{\underline{ID}\}) -\text{relationship} \rightarrow (\{CONCEPT\})$$

where ID is a column that uniquely identifies each row of the resulting query and is used as the identifier for Concept1.

Example 3.24

Source: The `sales_flat_order_payment_paypal` table stores all the payment transactions that came through the paypal payment platform.

sales_flat_order_payment_paypal	
entity_id	amount_paid
1	110
2	100

Target: The knowledge graph schema consists of the concepts *Order* and *PaymentMethod*. There are two types of payment methods: *Paypal* and *Visa* The relationship *hasPaymentMethod* connects the *Order* concept to one of the specific *PaymentMethod* types.

$$(\text{Order}) -\text{hasPaymentMethod} \rightarrow (\text{PaymentMethod})$$
$$(\text{Paypal}) -\text{type} \rightarrow (\text{PaymentMethod})$$
$$(\text{Visa}) -\text{type} \rightarrow (\text{PaymentMethod})$$

The expected knowledge graph is the following:

$$(\text{order-1}) -\text{hasPaymentMethod} \rightarrow (\text{Paypal})$$
$$(\text{order-2}) -\text{hasPaymentMethod} \rightarrow (\text{Paypal})$$

Mapping: To generate the knowledge graph, a constant value "Paypal," which is the same as the concept in the knowledge graph schema, is added to each row coming from the sales_flat_order_payment_paypal table. The mapping is the following:

```
SELECT entity_id, 'Paypal' AS method FROM sales_flat_order_payment_paypal
                                  ⟹
            (order-{entity_id}) −hasPaymentMethod→ (method)
```

This example is visually represented in Figure 3.24.

Discussion: Similar to Attribute Constant table.

3.4.6   RELATIONSHIP: CONSTANT ATTRIBUTE

Context: A column name in a table represents the value that needs to be mapped to a relationship and a corresponding concept.

Solution: Project the concept identifier from the table and filter by the column that represents the attribute. Provide a constant that the column is representing which is to be mapped to the Concept.

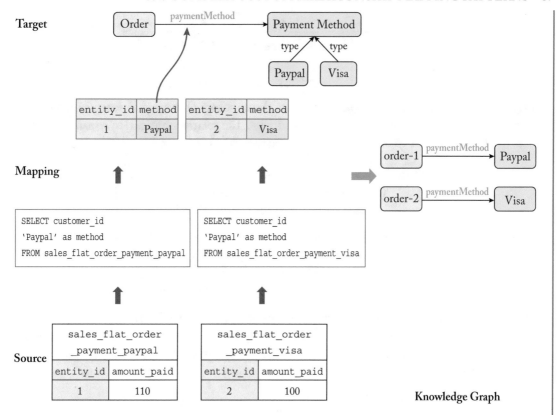

Figure 3.24: Relationship: constant table.

```
SELECT ID, 'CONSTANT' AS CONCEPT
FROM TABLE
WHERE CONSTANT = VALUE
                ⟹
(template-{ID}) −relationship→ ({CONCEPT})
```

where ID is a column that uniquely identifies each row of the resulting query and is used as the identifier for Concept1.

Example 3.25

Source: The sales_flat_order_payment table stores all the payment transactions and has a flag to know from which payment system it came from:

sales_flat_order_payment				
entity_id	amount_paid	paypal	visa	mc
1	110	1	0	0
2	100	0	1	0

Target: The knowledge graph schema consists of the concepts *Order* and *PaymentMethod*. There are two types of payment methods: *Paypal* and *Visa*. The relationship *hasPaymentMethod* connects the *Order* concept to one of the specific *PaymentMethod* types.

$$
\begin{array}{c}
\text{(Order)} -\text{hasPaymentMethod} \rightarrow \text{(PaymentMethod)} \\
\text{(Paypal)} -\text{type} \rightarrow \text{(PaymentMethod)} \\
\text{(Visa)} -\text{type} \rightarrow \text{(PaymentMethod)}
\end{array}
$$

The expected knowledge graph is the following:

$$
\begin{array}{c}
\text{(order-1)} -\text{hasPaymentMethod} \rightarrow \text{(Paypal)} \\
\text{(order-2)} -\text{hasPaymentMethod} \rightarrow \text{(Paypal)}
\end{array}
$$

Mapping: To generate the knowledge graph, a constant value "Paypal" is added to each row coming from the sales_flat_order_payment table where paypal=1, a constant value "Visa" is added to each row coming from the sales_flat_order_payment table where visa=1 , and so on. The mapping is the following:

Mapping for Paypal

```
SELECT entity_id, 'Paypal' AS method
FROM sales_flat_order_payment
WHERE paypal = 1
                ⟹
(order-{entity_id}) −hasPaymentMethod → (-{method})
```

Mapping for Visa

```
SELECT entity_id, 'Visa' AS method
FROM sales_flat_order_payment
WHERE visa = 1
                ⟹
(order-{entity_id}) −hasPaymentMethod → (-{method})
```

This example is visually represented in Figure 3.25.

Discussion: Similar to Attribute Constant Attribute.

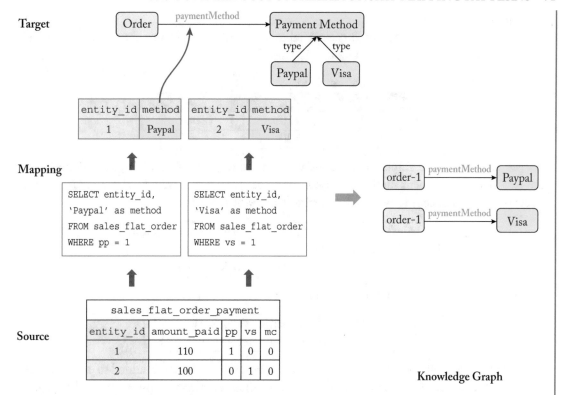

Figure 3.25: Relationship: constant attribute.

3.4.7   RELATIONSHIP: CONSTANT VALUE

Context: A value in a column is a code and it needs to be mapped to a Concept in the knowledge graph.

Solution: Project the concept identifier from the table and filter by value in the column that represents the Concept. Provide a constant that the value is representing which is to be mapped to the Concept

```
SELECT ID, 'CONSTANT' AS CONCEPT
FROM TABLE
WHERE type = 'CONSTANT'
                ⟹
(template-{ID}) −relationship→ ({CONCEPT})
```

where ID is a column that uniquely identifies each row of the resulting query and is used as the identifier for the relationship's associated concept.

Example 3.26

Source: The `sales_flat_order_payment` table stores all the payment transactions and has a flag to know from which payment system it came from:

sales_flat_order_payment		
entity_id	amount_paid	payment_type
1	110	pp
2	100	vs

Target: The knowledge graph schema consists of the concepts *Order* and *PaymentMethod*. There are two types of payment methods: *Paypal* and *Visa* The relationship *hasPaymentMethod* connects the *Order* concept to one of the specific *PaymentMethod* types.

$$(\text{Order}) - \text{hasPaymentMethod} \rightarrow (\text{PaymentMethod})$$
$$(\text{Paypal}) - \text{type} \rightarrow (\text{PaymentMethod})$$
$$(\text{Visa}) - \text{type} \rightarrow (\text{PaymentMethod})$$

The expected knowledge graph is the following:

$$(\text{order-1}) - \text{hasPaymentMethod} \rightarrow (\text{Paypal})$$
$$(\text{order-2}) - \text{hasPaymentMethod} \rightarrow (\text{Visa})$$

Mapping: To generate the knowledge graph, a constant value "Paypal" is added to each row coming from the `sales_flat_order_payment` table where `payment_type` = pp, and a constant value "Visa" is added to each row coming from the `sales_flat_order_payment` table where `payment_type` = vs. The mappings are the following:

Mapping for Paypal

```
SELECT entity_id, 'Paypal' AS method
FROM sales_flat_payment
WHERE payment_type = 'pp'
```
$$\Longrightarrow$$
$$(\text{order-}\{\underline{\texttt{entity\_id}}\}) - \text{hasPaymentMethod} \rightarrow (\text{method})$$

Mapping for Visa

```
SELECT entity_id, 'Visa' AS method
FROM sales_flat_payment
WHERE payment_type = 'vs'
```
$$\Longrightarrow$$
$$(\text{order-}\{\underline{\texttt{entity\_id}}\}) - \text{hasPaymentMethod} \rightarrow (\text{method})$$

This example is visually represented in Figure 3.26.

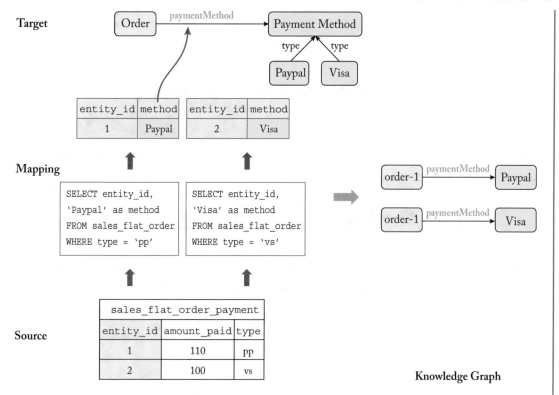

Figure 3.26: Relationship: constant value.

Discussion: This is a specific version of the CASE mapping pattern. Similar to Concept Attribute Constant Value.

3.4.8 RELATIONSHIP: BIDRECTIONAL

Context: A table represents a bidirectional relationship between two concepts. This is usually modeled by having two attributes (usually foreign keys) that reference the corresponding concepts that are being related. This means that the pair of attributes per row in the table represents an instance of the relationship between Concepts.

Solution: Create two mappings. The body of both mappings are the same. The head of each of the two mappings corresponds to the direction of the relationship between the two instances

$$\text{SELECT } \underline{\text{ID1}}, \underline{\text{ID2}} \text{ FROM TABLE}$$
$$\Longrightarrow$$
$$(\text{template1-}\{\underline{\text{ID1}}\}) -\text{relationship} \rightarrow (\text{template2-}\{\underline{\text{ID2}}\})$$

$$\boxed{\begin{array}{c} \texttt{SELECT \underline{ID1}, \underline{ID2} FROM TABLE} \\ \Longrightarrow \\ (\text{template2-}\{\underline{\text{ID2}}\}) - \text{relationship} \rightarrow (\text{template1-}\{\underline{\text{ID1}}\}) \end{array}}$$

where $\underline{\text{ID}}$ is a column that uniquely identifies each row of the resulting query and is used as the identifier for the relationship's associated concept.

Example 3.27

Source: The `customer_rel` table stores the social network between customers, when a customer connected with another customer:

customer_rel			
entity_id	customer_id1	customer_id2	created_at
10	1	2	2009-01-01

Target: The knowledge graph schema consists of the concepts *Customer* and the relationship *knows* connects a *Customer* concept with itself, thus it is a bidirectional relationship. If Customer A knows Customer B, then Customer B knows Customer A.

$$\boxed{(\text{Customer}) - \text{knows} \rightarrow (\text{Customer})}$$

The expected knowledge graph is the following:

$$\boxed{\begin{array}{c} (\text{customer-1}) - \text{knows} \rightarrow (\text{customer-2}) \\ (\text{customer-2}) - \text{knows} \rightarrow (\text{customer-1}) \end{array}}$$

Mapping: The knows relationship is bidirectional, meaning that if customer-1 knows customer-2, it implies that customer-2 also knows customer-1. To generate the knowledge graph, the knows relationship is mapped to the attribute ordered pairs (customer_id1, customer_id2) and (customer_id2, customer_id1). The mapping is the following:

$$\boxed{\begin{array}{c} \texttt{SELECT \underline{customer\_id1}, \underline{customer\_id2} FROM customer\_rel} \\ \Longrightarrow \\ (\text{customer-}\{\underline{\texttt{customer\_id1}}\}) - \text{knows} \rightarrow (\text{customer-}\{\underline{\texttt{customer\_id2}}\}) \end{array}}$$

$$\boxed{\begin{array}{c} \texttt{SELECT \underline{customer\_id1}, \underline{customer\_id2} FROM customer\_rel} \\ \Longrightarrow \\ (\text{customer-}\{\underline{\texttt{customer\_id2}}\}) - \text{knows} \rightarrow (\text{customer-}\{\underline{\texttt{customer\_id1}}\}) \end{array}}$$

This example is visually represented in Figure 3.27.

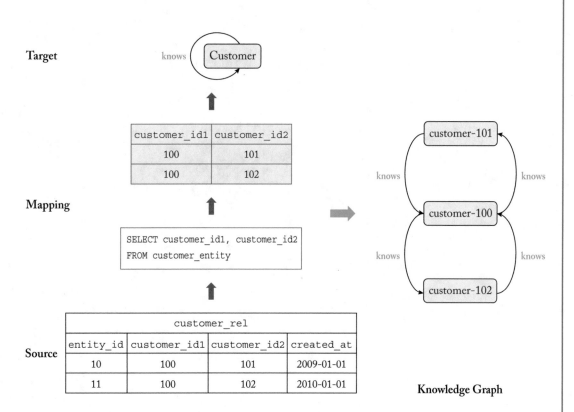

Figure 3.27: Relationship: bidirectional.

CHAPTER 4

Building Enterprise Knowledge Graphs

In the previous chapter, we defined the elements to design an Enterprise Knowledge Graph. We focused on mapping patterns that connect relational databases with knowledge graphs schemas. A natural question is: how to actually define the mappings in order to build the knowledge graphs? A common expectations is the existence of AI/ML technology that can generate these mappings.

However, the technology fallacy is *"the mistaken belief that just because business challenges are caused by digital technology, that they also need to be solved by digital technology"* [Kane et al., 2019]. If you put multiple people in a room, they will not agree on the meaning of a Customer. Furthermore, there will not be a consensus on which data should be used to identify a Customer. We are drowning in a sea of data, and it is clear that we need technology to help eliminate the noise, but if even humans do not agree on a meaning, why do we expect that AI/ML system will come up with the correct answer?

In order to build an Enterprise Knowledge Graph, we need to combine People, Processes, and Tools.

4.1 PEOPLE

Designing and building a knowledge graph is not just a technical task. It is important to understand who are the personas involved in the data ecosystem within an organization. The existing types of personas in an organization can be categorized as data producers and data consumers.

4.1.1 DATA PRODUCERS AND CONSUMERS

Data producers are responsible for managing the data infrastructure such as data warehouses, data lakes, data pipelines, etc. A data producer understands the database schemas and how the data are interconnected. For example, a data steward is responsible for a specific database, maintain its data dictionary, keep track of PII, and provision access to the data. A data engineer is responsible for the data infrastructure and builds the data pipelines that feed data into a lake. Other typical job titles of data producers are database administrator and ETL developer, among others.

Data consumers are responsible for analyzing data in order to answer business questions. They understand how the business functions, the important business questions that need to be answered, and work closely with subject matter experts. Traditionally, they will consume data from a data warehouse or a data lake. For example, a data analyst is responsible of creating and maintaining business intelligence report that answers business questions. A data scientist is responsible for finding trends in data by using statistical and machine learning methods. Other typical job titles of data consumers are BI developer and business analyst, among others.

Recall the problems described in Section 1.1. There is back and forth communication between data consumers and data producers when a data consumer requests data from a data producer. Think about the following questions.

- Did the data consumer communicate the correct message to the data producer?

- Did the data producer understand what the data consumer was requesting?

- Did the data producer deliver the correct data?

- Did the data producer generate the data in a repeatable manner? Or was it one-off work?

Common practice is that the data consumer receives data that needs to be further processed and cleaned. The famous 80/20 rule states: *"Most data scientists spend only 20 percent of their time on actual data analysis and 80 percent of their time finding, cleaning, and reorganizing huge amounts of data."*[1] This inefficient, repetitive process actually happens after the data producer delivers data to the data consumer. Clearly, there is a gap between the data producers and data consumers because the data lacks ownership.

4.1.2 DATA PRODUCT MANAGER

Let's step back for a moment and make an analogy with software. Software engineers and software users are bridged by product managers, who make sure that the software satisfies the requirements of the users. Now replace "software engineer" with "data producer," "software user" with "data consumer," and "software" with "data," and you'll see that the situation is analogous.

We need to treat data as a product. A *data product* is defined as a product that facilitates an end goal through the use of data [Patil, 2012]. Knowledge graphs enable data products. A data product can be the knowledge graph itself, or subsets of it. A data product can also be tabular view over the knowledge graph where the definitions from the knowledge graph are associated to each column of the tabular view.[2]

A product must have an owner who takes responsbility. A *data product manager* is responsible and takes ownership of data products. They understand the ecosystem of people and data,

---

[1]https://www.infoworld.com/article/3228245/the-80-20-data-science-dilemma.html
[2]Remember, data and knowledge needs to be connected and this can also be done in the form of a table.

and tasks in an organization that need to be addressed with the data. They manage a multi-disciplinary team responsible for producing, managing, exposing, and giving access to the data products.

From a social perspective, the team manages the shared business meaning, understands data consumers' requirements and use cases, and tracks the value that is being generated.

From a technical perspective, the team is responsible for maintaining the quality and reliability of the data through data wrangling, cleaning and provenance. This is much more than just eliminating white spaces, replacing wrong characters, and normalizing dates. This is about designing and building the knowledge graph schema and mappings which is the foundation of data products.

The work that a data product team does is what we call "knowledge science." Example scenarios are:

- lead conversations with your organization's stakeholders to understand their pain points,

- debate and document with stakeholders about the definition of a "customer" or "order net sales,"

- draw whiteboard sketches that define the schemas and models for data,

- maintain a data catalog,

- wrangle and clean data, and

- apply an agile methodology to generate data.

The team should constantly experiment and measure. Define KPIs metrics to track how the data products is being adopeted and used, and if it is driving ROI.

Therefore, a data product manager serves as the technical and communication bridge between Data Producers and Data Consumers. Members of a data product team have job titles such as knowledge scientist, knowledge engineer, ontologist, and taxonomist, among others.

4.2 PROCESS

Now that we have gone over the building blocks to design a knowledge graph, we need to understand the process to put those building blocks together in order to build the knowledge graph. The process we present is an agile methodology to create the knowledge graph schema and mappings in order to build a knowledge graph and data products in an iterative manner. Effectively, the knowledge graph will always continue to evolve. This process is based on the pay-as-you-go methodology [Sequeda et al., 2019].

Before starting the process, we need to define the success criteria. At the center of the methodology are a set of prioritized business questions that need to be answered, which serves as the success criteria for each iteration of the agile methodology. The business questions serve as competency questions that characterize the knowledge graph schema. The knowledge graph must be able to answer the business questions. If it does, then it was a successful iteration. If it doesn't, the iteration was not successful.

Even though the methodology is described assuming the schema is built from scratch, the schema can be bootstrapped by reusing an existing industry-specific knowledge graph schema. Ideally, one would hope that an existing knowledge graph schema fulfills the success criteria (i.e., prioritized business questions). If it does, reuse the portion of the existing knowledge graphs schema. If it doesn't, you can still be inspired by the existing knowledge graph schema.

Traditionally, the business questions fall under two categories.

- Business questions that take too long to be answered today: the process of answering business questions today takes too long because they follow ad hoc approaches (see "What is the Problem" Section 1.1).

- Business questions that have multiple and different answers today: depending on who you ask, the business question has different answers, hence there is a lack of trust.

The methodology is organized in three phases, with different expectations for each persona throughout the process.

Phase 1: Knowledge Capture The business question is analyzed and understood, resulting in a report that represents a minimal viable knowledge graph schema and mapping. A knowledge scientist discusses with data consumers to understand the business questions, define an initial "whiteboard" version of the knowledge graph schema and the expected data product that the data consumers want to consume. The knowledge scientist works with the data producer to determine which data is needed and define the SQL queries to access the data. These queries will ultimately become the mappings. This is documented in what we call a *knowledge report*.

Phase 2: Knowledge Implementation The knowledge scientist implements the knowledge graph schema and mappings based on the content of the knowledge report and generates the data product. The knowledge graph is validated to make sure it complies with the requirements established in the knowledge report.

Phase 3: Knowledge Access The data consumers are exposed to a data product. Tradition data tools (BI tools, R, etc.) can consume the tabular data product. Graph tools (graph analytics, graph visualizations, etc.) can consumer the graph data product. The data consumer can now use their preferred tools and provide answers to new and existing business questions without having to further interface with data producers.

Once this initial iteration is completed, the next business question is analyzed. If the next question can be answered with the current knowledge graph, then we are done. Otherwise, we might need to extend the knowledge graph schema and new mappings incrementally.

Table 4.1: Questions that need to be answered

	Questions
What?	What is the business problem? What are the business questions?
Why?	Why do we need to answer these questions? What is the motivation?
Who?	Who produces the data? Who will consume the data? Who is involved?
How?	How is this the business question answered today, if at all?
Where?	Where are the data sources required to answer the business questions? Are these databases? spreadsheets? or something else? How are data sources accessed?
When?	When will the data be consumed? Real-time? Daily? Update criteria?

With this approach, the knowledge graph is developed in an agile and iterative pay-as-you-go-approach. The following three sections will present each phase in detail. Section 4.2.4 will run through an e-commerce use case showcasing each of these phases through two iterations.

This methodology was developed and refined in projects with a number of customers, over several years. It builds upon the extensive work from the fields of knowledge acquisition and ontology engineering. Common steps across all methodologies is to identify a purpose, define competency questions and formalize the terminology in an ontology language [Uschold and King, 1995].

4.2.1   PHASE 1: KNOWLEDGE CAPTURE

The objectives of the knowledge capture phase are the following

- Understand and clarify the business questions,

- Identify the necessary data and queries to answer the business questions,

- Define the requirements of the data product.

Step 1: Analyze as-is Processes
The goal is to analyze and document existing processes because many of these processes may have never been written down before. When a business question needs to be answered, we first need to understand the larger context: what is the business problem that needs to be addressed? Is it currently being addressed, and if so, how? Answering the following questions, as shown in Table 4.1, help achieve this goal.

Table 4.2: Concepts in the knowledge report

Concept Name	The agreed label of a Concept
Concept Alternative Names	A list of alternative labels for the concept, including in different languages
Concept Definition	The agreed definition of a Concept
Concept Identifier	The identifier that will uniquely identify the Concept
Concept Instance Identifier	The attribute from the data that uniquely identifies each instance of the Concept and will form a global unique identifier
Table Name/SQL Query	The table name or SQL query that represents the Concept

Step 2: Collect Documentation

In this step, the knowledge scientist focuses on the answers to the How and Where questions from the previous step. They identify documentation about the data sources and any SQL queries, spreadsheets, or scripts being used to answer the business questions today. They may also interview data consumers and producers to understand their current workflow.

Step 3: Develop Knowledge Report

The knowledge scientist analyzes what was learned in steps 1 and 2 and starts working with the data consumers to understand the business questions, recognize key concepts, attributes and relationships from the business questions, identify the business terminology such as preferred labels, alternative labels, and natural language definitions for the concepts and relationships. At this stage, it is common to encounter disagreements. Different people use the same word to mean different concepts or different words are used to mean the same concept. These discussions and definitions need to be documented. The conversation is very focused on the business questions which helps drive a consensus. Subsequently, the knowledge scientist works with the data producers to identify which tables and attributes in the database contain data related to the concepts and relationships identified from the business questions. The conversation with the data producers is also focused.

An outcome of this step is a high-level overview of the knowledge graph schema: a whiteboard illustration. The final deliverable is a knowledge report detailing the Concepts, Attributes, and Relationships (CAR) of the knowledge graph schema. Each CAR is associated with SQL logic which serves as the mapping to the relational database. The template for the knowledge report is shown in Tables 4.2, 4.3, and 4.4.

The knowledge report also documents the tabular data products. A tabular data products is a table of data with columns that a data consumer would like to access in order to answer the original business question that kicks off the iteration of the methodology. The knowledge report

Table 4.3: Attributes in the knowledge report

Attribute Name	The agreed label of an Attribute
Attribute Alternative Names	A list of alternative labels for the Attribute, including in different languages
Attribute Definition	The agreed definition of an Attribute
Attribute Identifier	The identifier that will uniquely identify the Attribute
Associated Concept	The Concept for which this Attribute is associate to
Table Name/SQL Query	The table name or SQL query that represents the Attribute
Column	The column from the table/query that is the mapping to the Attribute
Datatype	The expected datatype of the Attribute
Attribute Cardinality	The expected cardinality: 1:1, 1:M of the Attribute
Nullable	If there are NULL values, what does it mean?

Table 4.4: Relationships in the knowledge report

Relationship Name	The agreed label of a Relationship
Relationship Alternative Names	A list of alternative labels for the Relationship, including in different languages
Relationship Definition	The agreed definition of a Relationship
Relationship Identifier	The identifier that will uniquely identify the Relationship
Associated From Concept	What Concept does this relationship come from?
Associated To Concept	What Concept does this relationship go to?
Table Name/SQL Query	The table name or SQL query that represents the relationships. This query should return a pair of attributes that represents the identifiers of the From and To Concept
Relationship Cardinality	The expected cardinality: 1:1, 1:M

for a tabular data product should list all the attributes of knowledge graph that will appear in the table.

The notion of Knowledge Reports mimics the Intermediate Representations (IRs) from METHONTOLOGY [Fernández-López et al., 1997]. In the conceptualization phase of METHONTOLOGY, the informal view of a domain is represented in a semi-formal specification using IRs which can be represented in a tabular or graph representation. The IRs can be understood by both the domain experts and the knowledge scientist, therefore bridging the gap between the data consumers informal understanding of the domain and the formal ontology language used to represent the domain.

The deliverable of this phase is the knowledge report, which documents how the business concepts are related, how they are connected to the data and the data products that the data consumers expect. The knowledge report needs to be peer-reviewed by the data consumers and data producers.[3] If all parties are in agreement, then we can proceed to the next phase. Otherwise, the discrepancies must be resolved. The discrepancies can be identified quickly due to the granularity of the knowledge report.

4.2.2   PHASE 2: KNOWLEDGE IMPLEMENTATION

A key insight of METHONTOLOGY's Intermediate Representations, is that they ease the transformation into a formal ontology language. We build upon this insight. That is why the goal of the knowledge implementation phase is to formalize the content of the knowledge report into a knowledge graph schema, mappings, and queries.

Step 4: Create/Extend Knowledge Graph Schema

Based on the knowledge report, the knowledge scientist can create the knowledge graph schema or extend the existing schema. This is straightforward to due given that knowledge report specifically documents the Concepts, Attributes, and Relationships of the knowledge graph.

For knowledge graphs implemented using RDF Graphs, Table 4.5 details the correspondence between the elements of the knowledge report and OWL ontology constructs.

Step 5: Implement Mapping

Similar to the previous step, the knowledge scientist can create the mappings from the knowledge report. The mappings express a correspondence from tables or SQL queries of the relational database to concepts, attributes and relationships of the knowledge graph schema. This implies that the complexity of creating mappings is left in SQL. After all, SQL is the most common query language.

For knowledge graphs implemented using RDF Graphs, Table 4.6 details the correspondence between the elements of the knowledge report and R2RML mapping constructs.

The mappings can be applied either in a virtualized (NoETL) or materialized (ETL) approach. In a virtualized approach, graph queries are translated to SQL queries using the mappings. In a materialized approach, the relational data is extracted, translated into a graph using the mappings and then loaded into a graph database.

---

[3]We peer review scientific papers. We peer review software code. We must also peer review the way we manage our data, in this case, the knowledge reports.

Table 4.5: Correspondence between knowledge report and OWL

Knowledge Report	OWL
Concept Name	Label (rdfs:label, skos:prefLabel) of owl:Class
Concept Alternative Names	Alternative Label (skos:altLabel) of owl:Class
Concept Definition	Definition (rdfs:comment) of owl:Class
Concept Identifier	IRI of the owl:Class
Attribute Name	Label (rdfs:label, skos:prefLabel) of owl:DatatypeProperty
Attribute Alternative Names	Alternative Label (skos:altLabel) of owl:DatatypeProperty
Attribute Definition	Definition (rdfs:comment) of owl:DatatypeProperty
Attribute Identifier	IRI of the owl:DatatypeProperty
Attribute Associated Concept	Domain (rdfs:domain) of owl:DatatypeProperty
Attribute Datatype	Range (rdfs:range) of owl:DatatypeProperty
Attribute Cardinality	An owl:Restriction
Relationship Name	Label (rdfs:label, skos:prefLabel) of owl:ObjectProperty
Relationship Alternative Names	Alternative Label (skos:altLabel) of owl:ObjectProperty
Relationship Definition	Definition (rdfs:comment) of owl:ObjectProperty
Relationship Associated From Concept	Domain (rdfs:domain) of owl:ObjectProperty
Relationship Associated To Concept	Range (rdfs:range) of owl:ObjectProperty
Relationship Cardinality	An owl:Restriction

Table 4.6: Correspondence between knowledge report and R2RML

Knowledge Report	R2RML
Concept Identifier	rr:class
Concept Table Name/SQL Query	rr:logicalTable
Attribute Identifier	rr:predicate
Column	rr:column
Attribute Table Name/SQL	rr:logicalTable, rr:sqlQuery
Relationship Identifier	rr:column
Relationship Table Name/SQL Query	rr:logicalTable, rr:sqlQuery

Step 6: Generate Data Products

Recall that tabular data product is the definition of the tabular result that a data consumer would like to access in order to answer their original business question. Graph query constructs such as SPARQL's SELECT, Cypher's RETURN, return tabular result set. Therefore, each tabular data product can be implemented by a graph query. The graph queries will then be executed over the resulting knowledge graph to generate the tabular data product.

Step 7: Validate Data

The final step in this phase is to validate the knowledge graph and the data products resulting in the queries from the previous step. This data should also be validated by both data producers and consumers. The validation should at least consider cardinality, counts, data types, missing values, and tabular data products.

- **Cardinalty**: The mapping report defined the expected cardinality for attributes and relationships. These cardinalities should be validated in the knowledge graph.

- **Counts**: Compare the number of results for each concept, attribute, and relationship with the number of results from the Table or SQL query on the relational database defined as the mapping. The number of results should be the same.

- **Missing Values**: Checking the validity of NULL values.

- **Tabular Data Product**: Share sample tabular data to the data consumer.

The cardinality, counts, and missing values validation can be implemented with graph queries and constraint/validation languages and thus automated. For RDF Knowledge Graphs, SHACL (Shapes Constraint Language) can be used to implement the constraints.[4] Traditional

---

[4]Recent tools such as Great Expectations could be adopted for this need.

data quality measures can be made (i.e., valid emails, valid dates, etc.), but that is out of scope for this book.

After successful data validation with the data producers and consumer, the data can begin to be used for Knowledge Access in the next phase. Otherwise, the root cause of the error must be found. This commonly occurs in either in the graph query or a mapping.

4.2.3   PHASE 3: KNOWLEDGE ACCESS

Step 8: Build Report

A goal is to enable data consumers to be self-service and answer their business questions. This is accomplished when data consumers can use analytics tools (BI tools, Graph visualization, etc.) over a simple and understandable view of the data. The knowledge graph enables the simplified view. Many data consumers will want to interact with the data using traditional BI tools that consume tables. This is why tabular data products are defined. Other data consumers will want to use advanced graph analytics tools, thus can consume the graph data product.

Step 9: Answer Question

The business report should answer the original business question (the "What" in Step 1). This report is shared with the stakeholders who asked the original business question (the "Who" in Step 1). If they accept the business report as an answer to their question, then this is ready to move to production.

Step 10: Move to production

Once the decision has been made to move to production, we need to determine how the knowledge graph will be managed. The options fall into two categories.

- **Virtualization:** The source relational database is accessed through virtual graph queries. This means that the graph queries in terms of the target knowledge graph are translated to SQL queries over the source relational database using the mappings. This provides up-to-date data. The viability of virtualization mainly depends on the use case and query access patterns.

- **Materialization:** The source relational database is extracted, transformed to graph using the mappings, and then loaded into a graph database.

We will discuss this more in the Tools section.

For each business question that is being answered, we need to determine how the data consumers and the reports will access the data. Can the reporting/analytics tool connect directly to a graph database? Or does it consume tabular data via SQL or imported tabular files (CSV/XLS). For a materialization approach, a refresh schedule for the tabular views must be determined. Common refresh schedules are daily, weekly, monthly, or on demand. Additionally, the time window of the extract needs to be determined. Is the entire knowledge graph going

Table 4.7: Questions in round 1

What	How many orders are placed in a given time period per their status?
Why	Depending on whom is asked, different answers can be provided. The IT department managing the website records an order when a customer has checked out. The fulfillment department records an order when it has shipped. The accounting department records an order when the funds charged against the credit card are actually transferred to the company's bank account, regardless of the shipping status. Unaware of the source of the problem, the executives are vexed by inconsistencies across established business reports.
Who	The Finance department, specifically the CFO.
How	A business analyst asks the data engineer for this information every morning.
Where	There is a proprietary Order Management System and an ERP system from a large vendor.
When	Every morning they want to know this number.

to be updated? Or is only yesterday's data going to be updated? Or last week's? These questions must be answered before wide release.

4.2.4   AN E-COMMERCE USE CASE

We present an example that goes through the methodology. We split the example in two rounds in order to see the nature of the agile methodology.

Round 1: Orders

Phase 1 (Knowledge Capture): We start by asking the questions in Step 1 above, and fill in the appropriate answers, as shown in Table 4.7.

The knowledge scientist gathers access to the database systems for the Order Management System and the ERP System and learns that the Order Management System was built on an open-source shopping cart system and has been heavily customized. It has been extended repeatedly over the past years and the original data architect is no longer with the company. Documentation about the database schema does not correspond to the production database schema. Furthermore, the database schema of the Order Management System consists of thousands of tables. Ten tables have the string "order" in the name with different types of prefixes (i.e., `masterorder`) and suffixes (i.e., `ordertax`).

The knowledge scientist gets the SQL script that the data engineer runs every morning to generate the data that is then passed along to a business analyst. It is important to call out that the data engineer did not write this SQL script; it was passed to them from a previous employee who is not at the company anymore.

The knowledge scientist works with data consumers to understand the meaning of the word "order." Discussions reveal that the definition of an order is if it had shipped or the accounts receivable had been received. Furthermore, with a view of the order number, order date and order status, the data consumers can answer their question. Together with the data engineer, the knowledge scientist learns that the Order Management System is the authoritative source for all orders because the ERP system consumes the data from the order management system. Within that database, the data relating to orders is vertically partitioned across several tables. The SQL scripts collected in the previous step provides focus to identify the candidate tables and attributes where the data is located. Only the following tables and attributes are needed from the thousands of tables and tens of thousands of attributes:

```
MasterOrder(moid, oid, master_date, order_type, osid, ...)
Order(oid, order_date, ...)
OrderStatus(osid, moid, order_status_date, ostid, ...)
OrderStatusType (ostid, status_type, ...)
```

The knowledge scientist working alongside the data engineer, identify the business requirement of an order as all rows in the `masterorder` table, where the `ordertype` column is equal to 2 or 3. Note that in some SQL scripts, this condition was not present. This is the reason why the Finance department was getting different answers for the same question.

Furthermore, it is revealed that the table `OrderStatus` holds all the different status that an order has across different periods of time. In discussions with the data consumer, it is confirmed that they only want to consider the last order status (they do not care about the historic order statuses). This may have been another source of differing numbers because a single order can have multiple order statuses, but it is unique for a given period of time. With this information, the knowledge scientist can whiteboard what the knowledge graph schema would look like.

Finally, an Order tabular data product is defined which consists of three attributes from the knowledge graph: Order Number, Order Date, and Order Status.

The Knowledge Report for Concepts are shown in Tables 4.8, 4.9, for Attributes are shown in Tables 4.10, 4.11, 4.12, for Relationships in Table 4.13, and for Data Product in Table 4.14.

Phase 2 (Knowledge Implementation): The knowledge scientist can now implement the knowledge graph schema. In our abstract notation, the knowledge graph schema is represented as follows:

Table 4.8: Order concepts in the knowledge report for round 1

Concept Name	Order
Concept Alternative Names	N/A
Concept Definition	An order is if it had shipped or the accounts receivable had been received
Concept Identifier	(Order)
Concept Instance Identifier	order-{moid}
Table Name/SQL Query	SELECT m.moid FROM masterorder m JOIN order o on m.oid = o.oid WHERE o.order_type in (2,3)

Table 4.9: Order status concepts in the knowledge report for round 1

Concept Name	Order Status
Concept Alternative Names	N/A
Concept Definition	An order can have a status
Concept Identifier	(OrderStatus)
Concept Instance Identifier	orderstatus-{osid}
Table Name/SQL Query	orderstatus

Table 4.10: Order date attribute in the knowledge report for round 1

Attribute Name	Order Date
Attribute Alternative Names	N/A
Attribute Definition	The date the order was placed on
Attribute Identifier	()-orderDate->[]
Associated Concept	(Order)
Table Name/SQL Query	SELECT m.moid, o.order_date FROM masterorder m JOIN order o ON m.oid = o.id
Column	order_date
Datatype	xsd:dateTime
Attribute Cardinality	1:1 an order must have exactly one order date
Nullable	There can't be NULL values. If there is a NULL value, then that is a data error

Table 4.11: Order number attribute in the knowledge report for round 1

Attribute Name	Order Number
Attribute Alternative Names	N/A
Attribute Definition	The unique number that identifies an order
Attribute Identifier	()-orderNumber->[]
Associated Concept	(Order)
Table Name/SQL Query	masterorder
Column	moid
Datatype	xsd:int
Attribute Cardinality	1:1 an order must have exactly one order number
Nullable	There can't be NULL values. If there is a NULL value, then that is a data error

Table 4.12: Order status label attribute in the knowledge report for round 1

Attribute Name	Order Status Label
Attribute Alternative Names	N/A
Attribute Definition	The label that an order status has
Attribute Identifier	()-orderStatusLabel->[]
Associated Concept	(OrderStatus)
Table Name/SQL Query	orderstatus
Column	label
Datatype	xsd:string
Attribute Cardinality	1:1 an order status must have exactly one label
Nullable	There can't be NULL values. If there is a NULL value, then that is a data error

Table 4.13: Relationships in the knowledge report for round 1

Relationship Name	has order status
Relationship Alternative Names	N/A
Relationship Definition	All orders have a status such as delivered, etc.
Relationship Identifier	()-hasOrderStatus->()
Associated From Concept	Order
Associated To Concept	Order Status
Table Name/SQL Query	SELECT moid, ostid, MAX(order_status_date) FROM orderstatus GROUP BY order_status_date
Relationship Cardinality	1:1 an order must have exactly one order status

Table 4.14: Order tabular data product in the knowledge report for round 1

Attribute	Concept
Order Number	Order
Order Date	Order
Order Status Label	Order Status

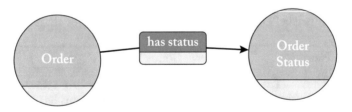

Figure 4.1: Knowledge graph schema.

```
(Order)
(OrderStatus)
(Order)-hasOrderStatus->(OrderStatus)
(Order)-orderNumber->[int]
(Order)-orderDate->[datetime]
(OrderStatus)-orderStatusName->[string]
```

Visually, the knowledge graph schema is shown in Figure 4.1.

In OWL, the knowledge graph schema is implemented as follows:

```
:Order rdf:type owl:Class ;
  rdfs:label "Order";
  rdfs:comment "An order is if it had shipped or the accounts
    receivable had been received";


:OrderStatus rdf:type owl:Class ;
  rdfs:label "Order Status";
  rdfs:comment "An order can have a status.";


:OrderDate rdf:type owl:DatatypeProperty ;
  rdfs:label "Order Date" ;
  rdfs:comment "The date the order was placed on.";
  rdfs:domain ec:Order ;
  rdfs:range xsd:dateTime ;


:orderNumber rdf:type owl:DatatypeProperty ;
  rdfs:label "Order Number" ;
  rdfs:comment "The unique number that identifies an order.";
  rdfs:domain ec:Order ;
  rdfs:range xsd:int ;


:orderStatusLabel rdf:type owl:DatatypeProperty ;
  rdfs:label "Order Status Label" ;
  rdfs:comment "The label that an order status has.";
  rdfs:domain ec:Order ;
  rdfs:range xsd:string ;


:hasOrderStatus rdf:type owl:ObjectProperty ;
  rdfs:label "has order status";
  rdfs:comment "All orders have a status such as delivered, etc.";
  rdfs:domain ec:Order ;
  rdfs:range ec:OrderStatus ;
```

The following is the mapping in our abstract notation:

$$
\begin{array}{c}
\texttt{SELECT } \underline{\texttt{moid}} \texttt{ FROM masterorder m} \\
\texttt{JOIN order o ON m.oid = o.oid} \\
\texttt{WHERE ordertype in (2,3)} \\
\Longrightarrow \\
(\text{order-}\{\underline{\text{moid}}\}) - \text{type} \rightarrow (\text{Order})
\end{array}
$$

$$
\begin{array}{c}
\texttt{SELECT } \underline{\texttt{osid}} \texttt{ FROM orderstatus} \\
\Longrightarrow \\
(\text{orderstatus-}\{\underline{\text{osid}}\}) - \text{type} \rightarrow (\text{OrderStatus})
\end{array}
$$

$$
\begin{array}{c}
\texttt{SELECT } \underline{\texttt{moid}} \texttt{ FROM masterorder} \\
\Longrightarrow \\
(\text{order-}\{\underline{\text{moid}}\}) - \text{orderNumber} \rightarrow [\{\text{moid}\}]
\end{array}
$$

$$
\begin{array}{c}
\texttt{SELECT } \underline{\texttt{moid}}\texttt{, o.order\_date FROM masterorder m} \\
\texttt{JOIN order o ON m.oid = o.oid} \\
\Longrightarrow \\
(\text{order-}\{\underline{\text{moid}}\}) - \text{orderDate} \rightarrow [\{\text{order\_date}\}]
\end{array}
$$

$$
\begin{array}{c}
\texttt{SELECT } \underline{\texttt{osid}}\texttt{, label FROM orderstatus} \\
\Longrightarrow \\
(\text{orderstatus-}\{\underline{\text{osid}}\}) - \text{orderStatusName} \rightarrow [\{\text{label}\}]
\end{array}
$$

$$
\begin{array}{c}
\texttt{SELECT } \underline{\texttt{moid}}\texttt{, ostid, max(orderstatusdate) FROM OrderStatus} \\
\texttt{GROUP BY orderstatusdate} \\
\Longrightarrow \\
(\text{order-}\{\underline{\text{moid}}\}) - \text{hasOrderStatus} \rightarrow [\text{orderstatus-}\{\underline{\text{osid}}\}]
\end{array}
$$

The following is the mapping in R2RML:

```
map:A a rr:TriplesMap ;
 rr:subjectMap [
  rr:class :Order ;
  rr:template "order-{moid}"
 ] ;
 rr:logicalTable [
   rr:sqlQuery """
```

```
    SELECT m.moid
    FROM masterorder m
    JOIN order o on m.oid = o.oid
    WHERE o.order_type in (2,3)
    """
].


map:A a rr:TriplesMap ;
 rr:subjectMap [
  rr:template "order-{moid}"
 ] ;
  rr:predicateObjectMap[
   rr:predicate :orderNumber;
   rr:objectMap [ rr:column "moid" ] ;
 ];
 rr:logicalTable [
   rr:tableName "masterorder"
 ].


map:A a rr:TriplesMap ;
 rr:subjectMap [
  rr:template "order-{moid}"
 ] ;
  rr:predicateObjectMap[
   rr:predicate :orderDate;
   rr:objectMap [ rr:column "orderdate" ] ;
 ];
 rr:logicalTable [
   rr:sqlQuery "SELECT m.moid, o.order_date FROM masterorder m
                JOIN order o ON m.oid = o.id"
 ].


map:A a rr:TriplesMap ;
 rr:subjectMap [
  rr:template "order-{moid}"
 ] ;
```

```
   rr:predicateObjectMap[
    rr:predicate :hasOrderStatus;
    rr:objectMap [ rr:template "orderstatus-{osid}" ] ;
  ];
  rr:logicalTable [
    rr:sqlQuery "SELECT moid, ostid, MAX(order_status_date)
                 FROM orderstatus GROUP BY order_status_date"
  ].

map:A a rr:TriplesMap ;
 rr:subjectMap [
  rr:template "orderstatus-{osid}"
 ] ;
 rr:predicateObjectMap[
   rr:predicate :orderStatusLabel;
   rr:objectMap [ rr:column "label" ] ;
 ];
 rr:logicalTable [
       rr:tableName "orderstatus"
 ].
```

The following graph queries generate the tabular data product:
SPARQL

```
SELECT ?Order_Number ?Order_Date ?Order_Status
WHERE {
?x a :Order;
  :orderNumber ?Order_Number;
  :orderDate ?Order_Date;
  :hasOrderStatus [
     :orderStatusLabel ?Order_Status;
  ]
}
```

Cypher

```
MATCH (o:Order)-[:hasOrderStatus]->(os:OrderStatus)
RETURN o.orderNumber, o.OrderDate, os.OrderStatusName
```

Gremlin

```
g.V().hasLabel('Order').outE('hasOrderStatus').
```

GSQL

```
SELECT Order.orderNumber, Order.orderDate, OrderStatus.orderStatusName
FROM Order-(hasOrderStatus)->OrderStatus
```

Sample data is provided to the data consumers and data producers for further validation.

Phase 3 (Knowledge Access): The knowledge graph is now accessible to the data consumers. Data consumers who want to consume a simple table can make use of the tabular data product with the reliable data that is needed in order to answer the original query: "How many orders were placed in a given time period per their status?" The tabular data product is now accessible to a large number of data consumers.

To get the exact same data directly from the database of the Order Management System, the data consumer would have to spend time with data producers to determine the SQL query, which would have been:

```
SELECT
    m.moid as OrderNumber,
    o.orderdate as OrderDate,
    ost.statustype as OrderStatusName
FROM masterorder m
JOIN order o ON m.oid = o.oid
JOIN (
    SELECT moid, ostid, max(orderstatusdate)
    FROM OrderStatus
    ROUP BY orderstatusdate
) os ON m.moid = os.moid
JOIN OrderStatusType ost ON os.ostid = ostid.ostid
WHERE m.ordertype in (2,3)
```

The need to write a query to access the data does not go away. The difference is that the graph queries are written in terms of the way how data consumers think about their domain. The SQL query is written in terms of the application which is completely separated from the data consumer's mental model. Being able to write queries, albeit graph queries, in terms of the data consumers mental model is the how the data-meaning gap is bridged, productivity is gained, and trust is earned.

Round 2: Order Net Sales

In order to demonstrate the agile nature of the methodology, consider the following new request: extend the knowledge graph with the net sales of an order.

Phase 1 (Knowledge Capture): In the first phase, the knowledge scientist needs to answer the key questions, as shown in Table 4.15.

In conversations with the data consumer, the knowledge scientist learns that the data consumer gets a CSV file from IT. The data consumer opens it in Excel and applies some calculations. The knowledge scientist works with the data consumer to understand the meaning of the word "order net sales." It is then understood that the net sales of an order is calculated by subtracting the tax and the shipping cost from the final price and also adjusting based upon the discount given. However, if the currency of the order is not in USD or CAD, then the shipping tax must be subtracted.

Working with a data engineer, they identify another table that is needed: `ordertax`. It is noted that the knowledge graph schema only needs to be extended to support two new Attributes: "Order Net Sales" and "Order Currency" associated to the Order concept as shown in the following knowledge report in Tables 4.16 and 4.17, respectively. The Order tabular data product is extended with those two new attributes as shown in Table 4.18.

Phase 2 (Knowledge Implementation): In our abstract notation, the knowledge graph schema is extended with the following:

```
(Order)-orderNetSales->[float]
(Order)-orderCurrency->[string]
```

In OWL, the knowledge graph schema is implemented as follows:

```
:orderNetSales rdf:type owl:DatatypeProperty ;
  rdfs:label "Order Net Sales";
  rdfs:comment "Subtracting the tax and shipping cost...";
  rdfs:domain ec:Order ;
  rdfs:range xsd:float ;
```

Table 4.15: Questions in round 2

What	What is the net sales of an order?
Why	Depending on whom is asked, different answers are provided. The net sales is dependent on at least 4 different aspects of each order and sometimes aspects of each individual line item. The departments and individuals reporting results are variously not applying all of the proper items, not applying them consistently or not applying them correctly (per the business' desired rules).
Who	The Finance department, specifically the CFO.
How	A business analyst asks the IT developer for this information every morning.
Where	This is in the proprietary Order Management System.
When	Every morning they want to know the net sales of every order and also various statistics and aggregations.

Table 4.16: Knowledge report for attribute order net sales

Attribute Name	Order Net Sales
Attribute Alternative Names	Revenue
Attribute Definition	Subtracting the tax and the shipping cost from the final price and also adjusting based upon the discount given. However, if the currency of the order is not in USD or CAD, then the shipping tax must be subtracted.
Attribute Identifier	()-orderNetSales->[]
Associated Concept	(Order)
Table Name/SQL Query	`SELECT moid, o.ordertotal - ot.finaltax - CASE WHEN o.currencyid in ("USD", "CAD") THEN o.shippingcost ELSE o.shippingcost = ot.shippingtax END as ordernetsales FROM masterorder m JOIN order o on m.oid = o.id JOIN ordertax ot on o.oid = ot.oids`
Column	ordernetsales
Datatype	xsd:float
Attribute Cardinality	1:1 an order must have exactly one order net sales
Nullable	There can't be NULL values. If there is a NULL value, then that is a data error.

Table 4.17: Knowledge report for attribute order currency

Attribute Name	Order Currency
Attribute Alternative Names	N/A
Attribute Definition	The currency in which the order was transacted
Attribute Identifier	()-orderCurrency0>[]
Associated Concept	(Order)
Table Name/SQL Query	order
Column	currency
Datatype	xsd:string
Attribute Cardinality	1:1 an order must have exactly one order currency
Nullable	There can't be empty currency. If there is a NULL, it is defaulted to USD

Table 4.18: Order tabular data product in the knowledge report for round 2

Attribute	Concept
Order Number	Order
Order Date	Order
Order Net Sales	Order
Order Currency	Order
Order Status Label	Order Status

```
:orderCurrency rdf:type owl:DatatypeProperty ;
  rdfs:label "Order Currency";
  rdfs:comment "The currency in which the order was transacted.";
  rdfs:domain ec:Order ;
  rdfs:range xsd:string ;
```

The following is the mapping in our abstract notation:

```
SELECT moid, o.ordertotal - ot.finaltax -
CASE WHEN o.currencyid in ('USD', 'CAD') THEN o.shippingcost
ELSE o.shippingcost = ot.shippingtax END as ordernetsales
FROM masterorder m JOIN order o on m.oid = o.id
JOIN ordertax ot on o.oid = ot.oids
```
$$\Longrightarrow$$
$$(\text{order-}\{\underline{\text{moid}}\}) -\text{orderNetSales} \rightarrow [\{\text{ordernetsales}\}]$$

```
SELECT moid, isnull(currency, 'USD') as currency FROM order
```
$$\Longrightarrow$$
$$(\text{order-}\{\underline{\text{moid}}\}) -\text{orderCurrency} \rightarrow [\{\text{currency}\}]$$

The following is the mapping in R2RML:

```
map:A a rr:TriplesMap ;
 rr:subjectMap [
  rr:template "order-{entity_id}"
 ] ;
 rr:predicateObjectMap[
   rr:predicate :orderNetSales;
   rr:objectMap [ rr:column "netsales" ] ;
 ];
 rr:logicalTable [
   rr:sqlQuery """
    SELECT moid, o.ordertotal - ot.finaltax -
     CASE WHEN o.currencyid in (''USD'', ''CAD'') THEN o.shippingcost
     ELSE o.shippingcost = ot.shippingtax END as ordernetsales
    FROM masterorder m
    JOIN order o on m.oid = o.id
```

```
      JOIN ordertax ot on o.oid = ot.oids
    """
 ].

map:A a rr:TriplesMap ;
 rr:subjectMap [
  rr:template "order-{moid}"
 ] ;
 rr:predicateObjectMap[
   rr:predicate :orderCurrency;
   rr:objectMap [ rr:column "currency" ] ;
 ];
 rr:logicalTable [
   rr:sqlQuery
     "SELECT moid, isnull(currency, 'USD') as currency FROM order"
 ].
```

The existing graph query are extended as follows:
SPARQL

```
SELECT ?Order_Number ?Order_Date ?Order_Status ?Order_Net_Sales
       ?Order_Currency
WHERE {
?x a :Order;
   :orderNumber ?Order_Number;
   :orderDate ?Order_Date;
   :orderNetSales ?Order_Net_Sales;
   :orderCurrency ?Order_Currency;
   :hasOrderStatus [
      :orderStatusLabel ?Order_Status;
   ]
}
```

Cypher

```
MATCH (o:Order)-[:hasOrderStatus]->(os:OrderStatus)
RETURN o.orderNumber, o.OrderDate, o.OrderNetSales, o.OrderCurrency,
```

```
        os.OrderStatusName
```

Gremlin

```
g.V().hasLabel('Order').outE('hasOrderStatus').
```

GSQL

```
SELECT Order.orderNumber, Order.orderDate, Order.OrderNetSales,
       Order.OrderCurrency, OrderStatus.orderStatusName
FROM Order-(hasOrderStatus)->OrderStatus
```

Phase 3: (Knowledge Access): With the extended Order tabular data product, the data consumers can further enhance the report in order to answer the new question of this round.

4.3   TOOLS

Building a knowledge graph and developing associated software that can consume graph data (and manage the graph) requires many different kinds of tools and software libraries. In this chapter we will discuss some of them, but the discussion is not "complete" from the standpoint of what is currently available, or as a tutorial on how to get things done. Rather than understanding specific tools (which come and go as the market evolves), it is more important to understand the kinds of tools one needs, and more specifically, how to evaluate them to be able to choose the ones that best suit one's needs.

4.3.1   METADATA MANAGEMENT

A first class of tools are for metadata management in order to create an inventory of your organization's data assets. The goals of these tools, also known as data catalogs are to:

- catalog what data assets (databases, tables, business terminology, reports, etc.) exist and how are they related to one another;

- understand and discover data assets related to topics and business concepts;

- provide governance to manage the policies related to data assets;

- describe provenance on how various data assets are related to one another over time; and

- enable collaboration between users and data assets.

A data catalog is a foundational tool to understand what data your organization has and how it could be effectively used to create a knowledge graph.

4.3.2   KNOWLEDGE MANAGEMENT

The data product team need to be equipped with knowledge managemenent tools to designing the knowledge graph. The following are the types of tools that would be used in Phase 1 of the methodology (Section 4.2.1).

Domain Modeling

Whatever data you manipulate or store, there is always a model (also referred to as a "schema" or "ontology"). Sometimes, this model is not explicit, but it exists nevertheless, at least in the developers' heads and is consequently reflected in the code that is written to manipulate or consume graph data. Some databases offer explicit support for representing a schema, although it should be noted that—at the time of writing—there is no widely accepted schema language for property graphs.[5] For RDF, representing a schema is always possible, as an RDF schema (or beyond that, an OWL ontology) is built and represented using basic RDF graph primitives. Thus, an RDF schema is embedded in, and coexists with, the graph's "instance" data, making RDF a particularly handy approach for "self-describing data."

To create a model, one needs some kind of an editor. Given that there are multiple textual serialization syntaxes for RDF,[6] one minimally needs a text editor (e.g., **Emacs**), but defining a larger model typically requires a dedicated editor. Some of these editors allow you to define the model graphically (e.g., **Gra.fo**) whereas others give you some type of structured "outline" view of your model (e.g., **Protégé**, **Topbraid**) or focus on taxonomies (e.g., **PoolParty**). Regardless, a model editor should be able to guide you in the definition of your model, whether that be by enforcing a valid model structure or beyond that, identifying inconsistencies in your model.

Schema Mapping

Once you have a model defined, it serves as the reference when defining other parts of your knowledge graph application. This includes the mappings from relational databases to the knowledge graph.

As discussed in Section 2.3.3, existing mapping languages are for RDF Knowledge Graphs. There are no known mapping languages for property graphs. At the time of writing, commercial tools include **Gra.fo and data.world**, **Metaphactory**, **Data Lens**, among others. Open source tools are **Karma**,[7] **RML**,[8] among others.

---

[5]At the time of writing, the Property Graph Schema Working Group of the Linked Data Benchmark Council is a community effort providing recommendations for a property graph schema language to the ISO GQL standards body.

[6]Turtle is the most common RDF syntax.

[7]https://github.com/usc-isi-i2/Web-Karma

[8]https://github.com/RMLio/rmlmapper-java

Typical functionality of schema mapping tools include mapping creation and editing either by writing "raw" R2RML or a visual paradigm, semi-automation of the mappings, and execution of the mappings in order to physically generate the knowledge graph.

Entity Resolution

Earlier, we spoke about the importance of good identifier conventions and schemes. *Entity resolution*[9] is the process of taking some description or mention of an entity and *resolving* it to a unique (pre-existing) identifier. Unique identifiers for entities (concepts and individuals) are the cornerstone for building working knowledge graphs, and entity resolution, typically as part of the graph ETL process, is thus an essential part of the process of building a knowledge graph. The accuracy of the entity resolution process also directly contributes to the overall data quality of your knowledge graph.

Entity resolution can range from a simple process of recognizing synonyms and picking a canonical name or identifier, to sophisticated matching involving machine learning techniques and even the use of a knowledge graph (say, DBPedia). Also, a common use case for knowledge graphs is *identity resolution* where, say, a company wants to identify a specific customer even though they have multiple different references (phone numbers, email addresses, actual names, etc.). This is a form of entity resolution.

Some sources of information about entity resolution are Herzog et al. [2007], Köpcke et al. [2010], and Getoor and Machanavajjhala [2012]. There are also a number of tools and libraries available for entity resolution, as well as cloud-based services, which fall under the traditional category of Master Data Management and Data Integration companies (e.g., Informatica, Talend, etc.).

4.3.3   DATA MANAGEMENT

The data product team need to be equipped with data management tools to build the knowledge graph. The following are the types of tools that would be used in Phase 2 of the methodology (Section 4.2.2).

Graph Databases

To build a knowledge graph one obviously needs some way of storing and managing the graph. At the time of writing, the graph database market is still very much nascent and in some ways the "Wild West," as there are a number of different query languages and graph (meta)models. There are some well-known and established graph database products (such as **Amazon Neptune**, **Stardog**, **Ontotext GraphDB**, **OpenLink Virtuoso**, **Neo4J**, **TigerGraph**, and **MarkLogic**) as well as a constantly changing landscape of newcomers. As an alternative to commercial and proprietary products, there are also open-source offerings that one should consider as possibilities; for example, all RDF frameworks and libraries typically offer some solutions for persis-

---

[9]Sometimes also referred to as *record linkage*, *reference matching*, *entity linking*, etc.

tence, whether those be "native"—a database implementation as part of the library—or solutions where the graph is backed onto some other type of third-party persistence substrate (relational database, key/value store, etc.).

The type of graph (meta)model one chooses limits the choice of query and schema languages available down the road. Most graph databases support either RDF graphs (and thus the SPARQL query language) or "labeled property graphs," or sometimes both. In the case of property graphs, two query languages have emerged that are not specifically tied to one single database implementation or product: Gremlin from the Apache Tinkerpop open source project and Cypher (specifically its open variant openCypher) from Neo4J. Besides those two, many database products have their own query languages or introduce extensions to existing query languages. Some database products also offer support beyond graphs, for document or relational storage.

Apart from the above, there is the choice between persistent databases and "in-memory" databases. In the case of the latter, one obviously needs some persistence solution from which the in-memory database can be (re-)populated when needed—this does not necessarily need to be a database, as the in-memory graph can simply be loaded from a static file, for example. In-memory databases are typically geared toward analytics and large-scale graph algorithm computation.

Graph Frameworks

Several open-source frameworks also offer solutions for persistence. For example, Java RDF frameworks **Eclipse RDF4J** (through its *RDF4J Server*) and **Apache Jena** (through its *Fuseki* server) both offer the option of persisting graphs on disk with access over HTTP. Similarly on the property graph side, **Apache Tinkerpop** offers the *Gremlin Server*. The RDF frameworks also offer "embedded" persistent graph database solutions (RDF4J through its `NativeStore` class, Jena through its `TDBFactory` factory class). For smaller applications, these approaches can be considered. Note, however, that most RDF frameworks typically rely on SPARQL and SPARQL Update and offer "wrappers" around graph databases that support these query languages.

Virtualization and Federation

When the relational data is highly dynamic or it is too big and not feasible to be materialized into a graph, it makes sense to virtualize the knowledge grah in order to keep the data in its original form. Research on translating SPARQL queries to SQL using mappings [Sequeda and Miranker, 2013] has matured over the past decade. This has led to various commercial offerings (e.g., data.world, Stardog, GraphDB, etc.). Additionally, there are open source offerings such as

Morph[10] [Priyatna et al., 2014] and Ontop[11] [Calvanese et al., 2017]. At the time of writing, there are no known virtualization tools for property graphs.

Federation provides the capability of aggregating knowledge graphs from distributed sources. The SPARQL query language for RDF knowledge graphs provides a federation extension to execute distributed queries over any number of SPARQL endpoints.[12] The SPARQL endpoint can be of an RDF graph databases or a virtualized knowledge graph over a relational databases. At the time of writing, there are no known federation tools for property graphs.

The combination of virtualization and federation enables accessing distributed knowledge graphs using a single query.

Other Databases

As we have learned, a graph is a mathematical construct—or, from the computer science standpoint, a data structure. Storing and managing a graph does not necessarily require a graph database per se, because graph structures can be stored using other database technologies as well. Depending on one's use case, this may or may not be particularly efficient, though.

The reason we bring up "other" databases is that they best serve our "knowledge graph exercise" as sources from which to populate a graph. That's really what this whole book is about, although we have mostly limited the discussion to relational (or tabular) sources. It should be noted, though, that document databases (e.g., **MongoDB**, **Amazon DocumentDB**), key/value stores (e.g., **Cassandra**, **Amazon DynamoDB**), and others, can also be used successfully. Finally, static data sources such as semi-structured data (e.g., XML documents) or structured data (e.g., CSV files) are also fair game when it comes to populating your graph.

Note, also, that populating your graph from external sources can take many forms: You can use the sources once, to initially construct your graph, or they can serve as the real "source of truth" and your graph is more like a cached version of that data; the latter case is obviously true for in-memory graph databases. If your source of truth is not the graph database, you may need to consider how changes to the graph—if allowed—can be propagated back to the source database.

Validation

W3C has produced a specification for validating RDF data, called SHACL (short for "Shapes Constraint Language"). In SHACL, a "shape" (rather than an RDF or OWL class) is a graph pattern against which graph data can be compared and validated. A shape is effectively a set of constraints that the graph data has to satisfy, and these shapes can be defined for nodes—and thus they roughly correspond to classes—or properties—in which case they correspond to property definitions or restrictions from RDF and OWL. In addition to being able to express and validate constraints that could be defined using OWL (e.g., cardinality constraints), SHACL also lets

---

[10]https://github.com/oeg-upm/morph-rdb

[11]https://github.com/ontop/ontop

[12]https://www.w3.org/TR/sparql11-federated-query/

one define constraints for syntactic validation of property values (e.g., to make sure that a string is formatted as a valid U.S. phone number).

There is also an alternative to SHACL, called ShEx (for "Shape Expressions"). Roughly similar to SHACL in functionality and capabilities, ShEx introduces a new syntax for expressing the shapes (SHACL shapes are expressed in RDF, and thus can co-exist in the broader graph they are meant to validate).

At the time of writing, there are no non-proprietary validation language for property graphs.

4.3.4   ADDITIONAL TOOLS

Search and Discovery

You have successfully created a knowledge graph and it is stored in a graph databases. The next step is to build data products using the knowledge graphs. These data products, let them be tabular, graphs or APIs, need to be searchable and discoverable by data consumers. Data Catalogs can be repurposed for this need. In addition to using a data catalog to inventory the raw data assets, they can be used to inventory the data products. Data producers are the audience of a data catalog of the raw data assets. On the other hand, data consumers are the audience of a data catalog of the data products derived from the knowledge graph.

Public Sources

Your knowledge graph can be enhanced and "enriched" by using public data sources. These sources include actual data (e.g., public knowledge graphs such as DBPedia, Wikidata) as well as public ontologies (such as Gist, FIBO, schema.org etc.).

For public data, you can either ingest that data into your graph, or you can use federated queries for access. For the former, you need to consider how to "refresh" the data if the public source is updated; for example, if you are using RDF, you can place the public data in a separate named graph, and perform "bulk updates" by deleting all data from that graph and reloading the external source. For the latter, you need to be prepared for potentially unanticipated changes in the public knowledge graph, or possible outages. Naturally, in both cases, you need to consider questions of trustworthiness, accuracy, etc., as well as legal questions such as usage rights.

CHAPTER 5

What's Next?

You are now asking how knowledge graphs relate to traditional movements and new trends:

5.1 COULDN'T I HAVE DONE THIS WITH A RELATIONAL DATABASE?

Yes. Technically, you can do whatever you want with a *Turing-complete language*. It's all just software. The question is if a relational database is the right technology to manage enterprise data and metadata. Recall, "The limits of my language mean the limits of my world." We have already been using relational database technology for almost half a century and we continue to experience this same conundrum. That is why we need to evolve enterprise data management.

5.2 ISN'T THIS JUST MASTER DATA MANAGEMENT?

Master Data Management (MDM) entails data integration of master data (customer, products, etc.). However, MDM is not a technology. It is considered a business discipline in which data consumers and data producers work together to ensure that an enterprise's master data assets are accurate and consistent. Therefore, MDM is one of the applications of Knowledge Graphs because it is a way to connect all your data together.

5.3 KNOWLEDGE GRAPHS AND AI

The goal of Artificial Inteligence—per some definition—is to build software agents that can display human intelligence. Inference, also called "reasoning," is traditionally a mechanism where via the application of *rules*—typically rules expressed in mathematical logic—graph data that is implicit can be made explicit, or where inconsistencies in your graph can be detected. For example, consider a graph containing information about people and their parents. Implicitly, the graph will reveal who people's grandparents are, but this information is not explicit. By defining that a "grandparent" is the "parent" of one's "parent," one can add "grandparent" edges to the graph and thus make this information explicit. Obviously, this is a very trivial example, but illustrates the point about implicit vs. explicit knowledge. This type of reasoning is called "symbolic", since it is based on the manipulation of symbols—in case of the example, the symbols include "parent" and "grandparent." "Non-symbolic" methods typically take the form of the application of statistical calculations to reveal implicit information or patterns in your data. Both types are discussed below.

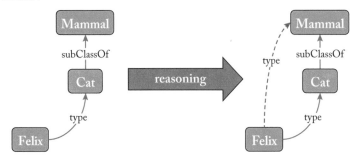

Figure 5.1: Simple example of entailment.

5.3.1 SYMBOLIC REASONING

The mechanisms for symbolic reasoning are defined for RDF graphs, by way of how the semantics of RDF Schema—RDF(S) for short—and OWL are defined.

RDF(S) is a simple ontology language which—in terms of logic—does not contain the notion of *negation*. This means that RDF(S) reasoning cannot create or reveal inconsistencies in your graph, it can merely add data. The added data—new edges in your graph—are called "entailments." RDF(S) establishes a simple object-oriented modeling system, with classes and subclasses, and can also organize property types (i.e., the kinds of edges you can have) hierarchically, as properties and "sub-properties." Reasoning mostly exploits the transitive nature of the subclass and sub-property relations: for example, if A is a subclass of B, and B is a subclass of C, we can infer that A is also a subclass of C, and so on. All this type of reasoning is "hard-wired" in RDF(S), so you cannot define any new relations that would be transitive, for example. See Figure 5.1 for a simple example of entailment in RDF.

OWL adds to the expressive power of RDF(S). For example, you can define new transitive relations, you can define a relation and its "inverse relation," and you can state that two nodes are, in fact, the same. As an example, if we define that "has-parent" is the inverse of, say, "has-child," then asserting that Bob has a parent called Alice allows the inference engine to conclude that Alice has a child called Bob.

The convenient characteristic of inference without negation is that you can establish a bigger, "virtual" graph that contains not only the original data but also all the entailments. Assuming you are running an inference engine either in your graph database or in front of it, your application code does in fact not need to know that inference is being performed. You merely query against the larger graph, whether that be virtual or whether the entailments have been physically materialized and added to the original graph.

Adding negation to the mix can complicate things from the application development standpoint. No longer can your application be ignorant about the existence of an inference engine, since inference may uncover conflicts or violations of constraints expressed in your model.

In OWL, negation comes in several forms: *Restrictions* are definitions of logical constraints that must hold, typically for the properties of a class in one way or another (e.g., the value of a property must always be of certain type, or there can only be at most one of a particular property). Other constraints include *disjointness* (e.g., the class of Cats and the class of Dogs are defined as disjoint, so the discovery of an instance that is both a Cat and a Dog is a violation of this constraint).

OWL specifications define several "profiles" for the language, with sligthly different semantics as well as different computational requirements and benefits. It is also very typical to employ something often referred to as "RDF+," an ad hoc mix of RDF(S) and some OWL features. Finally, some reasoning engines allow you to define "custom rules" to add to the reasoning capabilities of the system.

5.3.2 NON-SYMBOLIC REASONING

Reasoning does not have to be limited to classical, symbolic methods. If we consider the term more broadly, it can mean any methods by which we, say, uncover implicit information from the graph, or identify conflicts, constraint violations, or errors, in the graph. Reasoning is a way to enrich a knowledge graph, and this can be done by way of symbolic or non-symbolic inference (or even by purely procedural calculation and processing: sometimes this means the use of graph algorithms that consider the entire graph to calculate new, useful information about the graph).

Graph models and graph data are usually easy to understand, easier than corresponding relational models. Because of this, graphs can serve as input for machine learning models and make the work of data scientists easier. Results of machine learning, as suggested above, can be inserted back into the graph, creating a "virtuous cycle" of graph enrichment.

There are several books and articles that survey the landscape of ML and graphs, e.g., Hamilton [2020][1] and Nickel et al. [2016].

---

[1]The book [Hamilton, 2020] is available in pre-print form here: https://www.cs.mcgill.ca/~wlh/grl_book/.

CHAPTER 6

Conclusions

It's time to evolve the way we manage enterprise data! We need:

- to bridge the data-meaning gap between data producers and data consumers;

- data consumers' and business users' way of thinking about the world to be first-class citizens;

- the business concepts and relationships to be connected with the inscrutable application-centric relational databases; and

- to connect the data and metadata across an entire organization.

Knowledge graphs accomplish these goals.

6.1   IT'S ALL A GRAPH!

Everything is connected. Business concepts are connected with other business concepts. Disparate data sources can be linked together. The natural way of accomplishing these connections are through graphs. Thinking about RDF graphs versus property graphs is moot until you acknowledge that it is all a graph, and even then there is a lot of work (e.g., modeling your data as a graph) that is largely independent of your choice between the two graph models. The approach to designing and building knowledge graphs that we have presented in this book is applicable to both RDF and property knowledge graphs.

6.2   MAPPING PATTERNS

The connections between relational databases and knowledge graphs need to be accomplished in principled manner. Mapping patterns are a mechanism to apply reusable templates that solve a commonly occurring problem in order to prevent issues that may cause problems down the line.

6.3   YOU NEED A DATA TEAM

Success of designing and building a knowledge graph through an agile methodology depends on having a data product manager leading a team of knowledge scientists—data professionals with a broad set of technical and social skills. The data teams need to take responsibility of the data. Such people may be hard to find, and in our experience potential candidates have a technical background in data (SQL developers, etc.), know data modeling (UML, etc.), enjoy creating documentation, and regularly interact with business users. If looking internally, they are employees who have been at the organization for a long time and understand how the business functions. Potential candidates have dual backgrounds in computer science and arts (literature, music, etc.). The knowledge scientist serves as a communication bridge between data producers and data consumers to understand the meaning of data.

6.4   BE AGILE, START SMALL, DON'T BOIL THE OCEAN

It can sometimes take awhile to get the ball rolling but once data consumers see the first bits of understandable data they get excited and want more. Data consumers are empowered to ask questions that they had not even considered before with the status quo process. The agile process enables quickly adding more data in a way that data consumers can understand and easily access. The business benefit can be seen quickly and expanded. This feeds still more excitement for more data. The snowball gets larger and increasingly rolls down the hill faster. Additionally, executives can see tangible, early success and feels comfortable funding the activities or expanding funding.

Are you ready to change the way you manage your enterprise data?

Bibliography

Alexopoulos, P. (2020). *Semantic Modeling for Data*. O'Reilly Media, Inc. 31

Allemang, D., Hendler, J., and Gandon, F. (2020). *Semantic Web for the Working Ontologist: Effective Modeling for Linked Data, RDFS, and OWL*, 3rd ed., Association for Computing Machinery, New York. DOI: 10.1145/3382097 31

Azzaoui, K., Jacoby, E., Senger, S., Rodríguez, E. C., Loza, M., Zdrazil, B., Pinto, M., Williams, A. J., de la Torre, V., Mestres, J., Pastor, M., Taboureau, O., Rarey, M., Chichester, C., Pettifer, S., Blomberg, N., Harland, L., Williams-Jones, B., and Ecker, G. F. (2013). Scientific competency questions as the basis for semantically enriched open pharmacological space development. *Drug Discovery Today*, 18(17):843–852. DOI: 10.1016/j.drudis.2013.05.008 15

Berners-Lee, T., Hendler, J., and Lassila, O. (2001). The semantic web. *Scientific American*, 284(5):34–43. DOI: 10.1038/scientificamerican0501-34 14, 20

Bonifati, A., Fletcher, G. H. L., Voigt, H., and Yakovets, N. (2018). *Querying Graphs*. Synthesis Lectures on Data Management. Morgan & Claypool Publishers. DOI: 10.2200/s00873ed1v01y201808dtm051 25

Brachman, R. J. (1979). On the epistemological status of semantic networks. In Findler, N., Ed., *Associative Networks: Representation and Use of Knowledge by Computers*, pages 3–50, Academic Press, New York. 13
DOI: 10.1016/b978-0-12-256380-5.50007-4

Brachman, R. J. and Levesque, H. J., Eds. (1985). *Readings in Knowledge Representation*. Morgan Kaufmann, San Mateo, CA. 12

Calvanese, D., Cogrel, B., Komla-Ebri, S., Kontchakov, R., Lanti, D., Rezk, M., Rodriguez-Muro, M., and Xiao, G. (2017). Ontop: Answering SPARQL queries over relational databases. *Semantic Web*, 8(3):471–487. DOI: 10.3233/sw-160217 127

Codd, E. F. (1970). A relational model of data for large shared data banks. *Communications of the ACM*, 13(6):377–387. DOI: 10.1145/362384.362685 19

Corcho, O., Fernández-López, M., and Gómez-Pérez, A. (2003). Methodologies, tools and languages for building ontologies. Where is their meeting point? *Data and Knowledge Engineering*, 46(1):41–64. DOI: 10.1016/s0169-023x(02)00195-7 15

Euler, L. (1736). Solutio problematis ad geometriam situs pertinentis. *Commentarii Academiae Scientiarum Imperialis Petropolitanae*, 8:128–140. 12

Fernández-López, M., Gómez-Pérez, A., and Juristo, N. (1997). Methontology: From ontological art towards ontological engineering. *AAAI-97 Spring Symposium Series*, Stanford University, March 24–26. 15, 103

Fikes, R. and Kehler, T. (1985). The role of frame-based representation in reasoning. *Communications of the ACM*, 28(9):904–920. DOI: 10.1145/4284.4285 13

Fox, M. S. and Grüninger, M. (1997). Ontologies for enterprise modelling. In *Enterprise Engineering and Integration*, pages 190–200, Springer. DOI: 10.1007/978-3-642-60889-6_22 15

Getoor, L. and Machanavajjhala, A. (2012). Entity resolution: Theory, practice and open challenges. *Proc. of the VLDB Endowment*, 5(12):2018–2019. DOI: 10.14778/2367502.2367564 125

Goodhue, D. L., Wybo, M. D., and Kirsch, L. J. (1992). The impact of data integration on the costs and benefits of information systems. *MIS Quarterly*, 16(3):293–311. DOI: 10.2307/249530 1

Gutierrez, C. and Sequeda, J. F. (2021). Knowledge graphs. *Communications of the ACM*, 64(3):96–104. DOI: 10.1145/3418294 2, 13

Hamilton, W. L. (2020). Graph representation learning. *Synthesis Lectures on Artificial Intelligence and Machine Learning*, 14(3):1–159. DOI: 10.2200/s01045ed1v01y202009aim046 131

Hayes, P. J. (1974). Some problems and non-problems in representation theory. In *Proc. of the AISB Summer Conference*, pages 63–79, University of Sussex. 13

Hendler, J. and Golbeck, J. (2008). Metcalfe's law, Web 2.0, and the semantic web. *Journal of Web Semantics*, 6(1):14–20. DOI: 10.1016/j.websem.2007.11.008 27

Herzog, T. N., Scheuren, F. J., and Winkler, W. E. (2007). *Data Quality and Record Linkage Techniques*. Springer Science and Business Media. DOI: 10.1007/0-387-69505-2 125

Hitzler, P., Gangemi, A., Janowicz, K., Krisnadhi, A., and Presutti, V., Eds. (2016). *Ontology Engineering with Ontology Design Patterns—Foundations and Applications*, vol. 25 of *Studies on the Semantic Web*. IOS Press. 15

Inmon, W. H. (2005). *Building the Data Warehouse*, 4th ed., John Wiley & Sons, Inc. 5

Jiménez-Ruiz, E., Kharlamov, E., Zheleznyakov, D., Horrocks, I., Pinkel, C., Skjæveland, M. G., Thorstensen, E., and Mora, J. (2015). Bootox: Practical mapping of RDBS to OWL 2. In Arenas, M., Corcho, Ó., Simperl, E., Strohmaier, M., d'Aquin, M., Srinivas, K., Groth, P., Dumontier, M., Heflin, J., Thirunarayan, K., and Staab, S., Eds., *The Semantic Web— ISWC 2015—14th International Semantic Web Conference, Bethlehem, PA, October 11–15, 2015, Proceedings, Part II*, vol. 9367 of *Lecture Notes in Computer Science*, pages 113–132, Springer. DOI: 10.1007/978-3-319-25010-6_7 16

Kane, G., Phillips, A., Copulsky, J., and Andrus, G. (2019). *The Technology Fallacy: How People are the Real Key to Digital Transformation*. Management on the Cutting Edge, MIT Press. DOI: 10.7551/mitpress/11661.001.0001 97

Karp, P. D. (1992). The design space of frame knowledge representation systems. *Technical Report 520*, SRI International Artificial Intelligence Center. 13

Keet, C. M. and Lawrynowicz, A. (2016). Test-driven development of ontologies. In Sack, H., Blomqvist, E., d'Aquin, M., Ghidini, C., Ponzetto, S. P., and Lange, C., Eds., *The Semantic Web. Latest Advances and New Domains—13th International Conference, ESWC 2016, Heraklion, Crete, Greece, May 29–June 2, 2016, Proceedings*, vol. 9678 of *Lecture Notes in Computer Science*, pages 642–657, Springer. DOI: 10.1007/978-3-319-34129-3_39 15

Kendall, E. F. and McGuinness, D. L. (2019). *Ontology Engineering*. Synthesis Lectures on the Semantic Web: Theory and Technology. Morgan & Claypool Publishers. DOI: 10.2200/s00834ed1v01y201802wbe018 15

Köpcke, H., Thor, A., and Rahm, E. (2010). Evaluation of entity resolution approaches on real-world match problems. *Proc. of the VLDB Endowment*, 3(1–2):484–493. DOI: 10.14778/1920841.1920904 125

M. Arenas, A. Bertails, E. P. J. S. (2012). A direct mapping of relational data to RDF. *Technical Report*, W3C Recommendation. 34

McComb, D. (2018). *Software Wasteland: How the Application-Centric Mindset is Hobbling our Enterprises*. Technics Publications. 11

McComb, D. (2019). *The Data-Centric Revolution: Restoring Sanity to Enterprise Information Systems*. Technics Publications. 9

Minsky, M. (1975). A framework for representing knowledge. In Winston, P. H., Ed., *Psychology of Computer Vision*. McGraw-Hill, New York. 13

Nickel, M., Murphy, K., Tresp, V., and Gabrilovich, E. (2016). A review of relational machine learning for knowledge graphs. *Proc. of the IEEE*, 104(1):11–33. DOI: 10.1109/jproc.2015.2483592 131

Noy, N. F., Gao, Y., Jain, A., Narayanan, A., Patterson, A., and Taylor, J. (2019). Industry-scale knowledge graphs: Lessons and challenges. *Communications of the ACM*, 62(8):36–43. DOI: 10.1145/3331166 12

Patil, D. (2012). *Data Jujitsu: The Art of Turning Data into Product—Kindle Edition*. O'Reilly Media. 98

Priyatna, F., Corcho, Ó., and Sequeda, J. F. (2014). Formalisation and experiences of R2RML-based SPARQL to SQL query translation using morph. In Chung, C., Broder, A. Z., Shim, K., and Suel, T., Eds., *23rd International World Wide Web Conference, WWW'14, Seoul, Republic of Korea, April 7–11, 2014*, pages 479–490, ACM. DOI: 10.1145/2566486.2567981 127

Quillian, M. R. (1967). Word concepts: A theory and simulation of some basic semantic capabilities. *Behavioral Science*, 12:410–430. DOI: 10.1002/bs.3830120511 13

Ren, Y., Parvizi, A., Mellish, C., Pan, J. Z., van Deemter, K., and Stevens, R. (2014). Towards competency question-driven ontology authoring. In Presutti, V., d'Amato, C., Gandon, F., d'Aquin, M., Staab, S., and Tordai, A., Eds., *The Semantic Web: Trends and Challenges—11th International Conference, ESWC 2014, Anissaras, Crete, Greece, May 25–29, 2014. Proceedings*, vol. 8465 of *Lecture Notes in Computer Science*, pages 752–767, Springer. DOI: 10.1007/978-3-319-07443-6_50 15

S. Das, S. Sundara, R. C. (2012). R2RML: RDB to RDF mapping language. *Technical Report*, W3C Recommendation. 41, 42

Sequeda, J. F., Arenas, M., and Miranker, D. P. (2012). On directly mapping relational databases to RDF and OWL. In Mille, A., Gandon, F. L., Misselis, J., Rabinovich, M., and Staab, S., Eds., *Proc. of the 21st World Wide Web Conference, WWW 2012*, pages 649–658, ACM, Lyon, France, April 16–20. DOI: 10.1145/2187836.2187924 16, 32

Sequeda, J. F., Briggs, W. J., Miranker, D. P., and Heideman, W. P. (2019). A pay-as-you-go methodology to design and build enterprise knowledge graphs from relational databases. In Ghidini, C., Hartig, O., Maleshkova, M., Svátek, V., Cruz, I. F., Hogan, A., Song, J., Lefrançois, M., and Gandon, F., Eds., *The Semantic Web—ISWC 2019—18th International Semantic Web Conference, Auckland, New Zealand, October 26–30, 2019, Proceedings, Part II*, vol. 11779 of *Lecture Notes in Computer Science*, pages 526–545, Springer. DOI: 10.1007/978-3-030-30796-7_32 99

Sequeda, J. F. and Miranker, D. P. (2013). Ultrawrap: SPARQL execution on relational data. *Journal of Semantics*, 22:19–39. DOI: 10.1016/j.websem.2013.08.002 126

Suárez-Figueroa, M. C., Gómez-Pérez, A., Motta, E., and Gangemi, A., Eds. (2012). *Ontology Engineering in a Networked World*. Springer. DOI: 10.1007/978-3-642-24794-1 15

Tudorache, T. (2020). Ontology engineering: Current state, challenges, and future directions. *Semantic Web*, 11(1):125–138. DOI: 10.3233/sw-190382 15

Uschold, M. (2018). *Demystifying OWL for the Enterprise.* Synthesis Lectures on the Semantic Web: Theory and Technology. Morgan & Claypool Publishers. DOI: 10.2200/s00824ed1v01y201801wbe017 22

Uschold, M. and King, M. (1995). *Towards a Methodology for Building Ontologies*. Citeseer. 15, 101

Woods, W. A. (1975). What's in a link: Foundations of semantic networks. In D. G. Bobrow and A. M. Collins, Eds., *Representation and Understanding: Studies in Cognitive Science*, pages 35–82, Academic Press, New York. DOI: 10.1016/B978-0-12-108550-6.50007-0 13

Authors' Biographies

JUAN SEQUEDA

Juan Sequeda is the Principal Scientist at data.world. He joined through the acquisition of Capsenta, a company he founded as a spin-off from his research. Juan's goal is to reliably create knowledge from inscrutable data. His academic and industry work has been on designing and building knowledge graphs for enterprise data integration where he has researched and developed technologies for semantic and graph data virtualization, ontology and graph data modeling and schema mapping, and data integration methodologies.

Juan serves as a bridge between academia and industry through standardization committees, like serving as the co-chair of the Property Graph Schema Working Group and a past member of the Graph Query Languages task force of the Linked Data Benchmark Council (LDBC), as well as a past invited expert member and standards editor at the World Wide Web Consortium (W3C).

Juan holds a Ph.D. in Computer Science from The University of Texas at Austin. He is the recipient of the NSF Graduate Research Fellowship, 2nd place in the 2013 Semantic Web Challenge for his work on ConstituteProject.org, Best Student Research Paper at International Semantic Web Conference 2014, and the 2015 Best Transfer and Innovation Project awarded by the Institute for Applied Informatics.

ORA LASSILA

Ora Lassila is a Principal Graph Technolgist in the Amazon Neptune graph database team. Earlier, he was a Managing Director at State Street, heading efforts to adopt ontologies and graph databases. Before that, he worked as a technology architect at Pegasystems, as an architect and technology strategist at Nokia Location & Commerce (later renamed HERE), and prior to that as a Research Fellow at the Nokia Research Center. He was an elected member of the Advisory Board of the World Wide Web Consortium (W3C) in 1998–2013, and represented Nokia in the W3C Advisory Committee in 1998–2002. In 1996–1997 he was a Visiting Scientist at MIT Laboratory for Computer Science, working with W3C and launching the Resource Description Framework (RDF) standard; he served as a co-editor of the original RDF Model and Syntax specification.

Much of his research work at the Nokia Research Center focused on the Semantic Web and particularly its applications to mobile and ubiquitous computing. He collaborated with several U.S. universities, and was an active participant in the DARPA Agent Markup Language (DAML) program.

His positions before that include Project Manager at the Robotics Institute of Carnegie Mellon University and Research Scientist at the Computer Science Laboratory of Helsinki University of Technology. He has also worked as a software engineer in several companies (including his own start-up). He is the author of more than 100 conference papers and journal articles. He holds a Ph.D. in Computer Science from the Helsinki University of Technology (renamed Aalto University some years ago). Ora is the recipient of the Best Student Paper award of the 1989 Scandinavian Conference on AI, the Grand Prize of the 1989 Usenix Obfuscated C Code Contest, and the Semantic Web Science Association's 10-year award.

Printed in the United States
by Baker & Taylor Publisher Services